Is This Love?

Is This Love?

c. e. riley

First published in Great Britain in 2022 by Serpent's Tail,
an imprint of PROFILE BOOKS LTD
29 Cloth Fair
London
EC1A 7JQ
www.serpentstail.com

10 9 8 7 6 5 4 3 2 1

Designed by Crow Books
Printed and bound in Great Britain by Clays Ltd, Elcograf S.p.A.

A CIP record for this book can be obtained from the British Library

ISBN: 978 1 80081 0280
eISBN: 978 1 8283 9750

I dedicate this story to anyone who recognises themselves in this story. And who got through it.

November

'I'm divorcing you,' you said.

'You can't divorce me. We're married,' I said, not grasping my best arguments straight off the bat.

'I've been to see a solicitor, and I've started proceedings. There's nothing you can do to stop me.'

I felt something deeper than panic rise from the pit of my stomach. 'What are you talking about? You can't just start divorcing someone without a conversation.' I moved to stand between you and the door.

'Get out of my way, I'm going to work.'

'Are you fucking mad?' I said, my voice rising. 'You're going to work? You've just told me we're getting a divorce and now you're going to work?'

The calm in your voice was a provocation. I knew it, but just as I always did, I responded. Just as you knew I would.

'I'm not going to have you scream at me,' you said, a long-suffering parent scolding an errant child. 'I've told you what I'm doing. Now it's up to you to sort yourself out.'

I took a step towards you. You moved away. Here it was, the inevitable dance. We'd been here before, me begging, you cold and unmoved. I hated myself even as I repeated the steps.

'I'm not screaming,' I said. 'I just want to talk. You don't have to do this. It's crazy. Things aren't that bad. I can change, I've said that. I'll do whatever you want. I've said that too. There's too much that's good between us for you to just walk out like this.'

I watched you. You didn't blink. The panic in my chest turned to a cold, hard dread. I felt sure that there was something I could say to stop you, but I couldn't think fast enough to come up with the words. And there was a darkness creeping in at the corner of my vision that threatened to block out this entire scene, to render me blind and stumbling and alone.

'Please,' I said. 'Please don't. I love you. I've never loved anyone like I love you.'

And it was true. I had jumped head first into our relationship like a lovelorn teenager. You had made me feel like a conquering hero; you'd told me that what we had was a miracle. And I'd believed you, completely seduced by the story of us, by the way you'd constructed me as the lover you'd never believed would come along.

The first time I kissed you, we were sitting on our friend's bed, upstairs at a party. I'd gone up to find a drink, or a line, or a packet of cigarettes, and there you were, waiting. Smiling. You'd been smiling earlier, too, when I noticed you dancing, grinning among our friends in the tightly packed living room. I'd been hoping to catch you alone, to test the waters. And you'd made it so easy for me, waiting in the bedroom with that smile, those eyes. A few playful sentences and then you leaned over. One long kiss, then another. You danced up and away from me, and we headed downstairs like foolish teenagers. I knew you wanted more. I played it cool, and saw you off from the party, sneaking into the front garden to sink into another deep kiss before you waved goodbye. I was already under your spell.

On our first date, a warm night in April, I took you to dinner at the top of one of London's towers. We sat with the city at our feet, smiling at one another, and ate overpriced food in the company of tourists and city folk and media men. I didn't taste any of it.

I couldn't afford that meal, but I was showing off. I wanted to show you off.

You wore a jumpsuit, jet black, with a silver belt across your flat stomach. I marvelled at your cheekbones, the chiselled line of your jaw: strong and sculptured. Your hair, jet black too, was cut into a bob with a sharp fringe. It hadn't yet lost its sheen. You'd drawn an emerald-green line across your upper eyelids, which gave you the look of an Egyptian princess. Or so I thought. I used to think those things of you then. The pedestal I'd put you on meant it was hard to see you clearly.

We left the restaurant and walked along the river hand in hand. Already, it felt like you were mine. I threw sideways looks at you, disbelieving my own good luck. I thought you were beautiful.

You were beautiful.

As the summer arrived, nights turned into whole weekends. How quickly I made my confession of love to you. And you to me.

I couldn't stop myself. I was swept up in the romance of us. I saw strangers smiling at us as we walked by them, waiters ushered us to the best tables, the radio played our songs and the weather stayed idyllic, the evenings long and the nights hot.

We slept little. It seemed a waste of time. Your desire for me swelled my ego and my libido, and you wouldn't let me rest, nor I you. You clawed me into you as you came, dragging red lines down my back, making me cry out. I wore them like a badge of honour, grinning idiotically to myself as I lifted my T-shirt in gym changing rooms, turning to face the wall to better show off my prize. Your love always did hurt.

We started spending every night together. And when we couldn't see each other at the end of the day, you'd come to my flat in the early morning, and we'd have sex instead of breakfast and you'd leave with tangled hair and a lingering kiss. You were thrilled when a colleague told you how well you looked, that you were glowing. We laughed about it, conspirators in our story, keeping our secret.

We came out to the friends of ours that were mutual, slowly, one by one. They smiled, and looked awkward as we held hands under the table and made excuses to leave early.

You talked to me of previous lovers, saying you weren't in touch with any of them. I bristled as you described those relationships, and how they'd gone wrong. How you'd been wronged. How could anyone have hurt *you*? I wondered. Aloud, I said it was my brilliant luck that had kept you for me. I didn't think to question how you'd got to your fourth decade without any ghosts from your past still present. I had so many. Mostly they were benign.

You told me about your work as a counsellor, your specialist work with the dying. I thought you were an angel. Comforting frightened souls as they approached the end. It was an impression you were happy to cultivate. You demurred as I praised you, so brave in readying them for an ending. I didn't know then that endings meant so little to you.

I swooned at this kind, open-hearted ideal, picturing you tending to the desperate before coming home to tend to me. I hadn't realised how desperate I was for some attention. I had been on my own for a long time, and while I'd told myself I was having fun – I *was* having fun – being single was also brutalising in small, specific ways. The dating scene bruised me: I was always too hurt when women didn't call back. I felt selfish and mean when I didn't call them. And I missed being sure: that I was wanted, that I was thought of. Sure that I wouldn't be on my own for another weekend, the single funster in a group of coupled-up committeds. It was so *nice* to be part of that comfortable structure of two once again. I felt safer, and calmer, and happy.

I was happy.

The summer months flew by. As autumn arrived, I started teaching. I was finding my way into an academic career, nosing a route into a part-time post on the very bottom rung of the ladder. I was excited; it felt like the start of something. Everything was coming together at once. I had my friends, my flat, my work. And I had you.

You came to meet me at the end of my first week, and I could barely keep my hands off you as we walked away from campus. I must have looked like a horny student rather than a member of the faculty. Do you remember how stupidly in love we were? You told me I made you think of the first time you'd tasted cherryade: a deliciousness you didn't expect, the surprise of the new. Sweet and bright and just enough sour to keep you interested. I'd loved that. I bought you a bottle of it from the corner shop. You never drank it. We kept it in the fridge door. Do you remember that? It was still there, the day you walked out.

By Christmas that first year, things stepped up a gear. You said your flat was up for sale: the council wanted to purchase it compulsorily, part of a grand redevelopment plan. The beginning of the end of Hackney. You'd lived in the flat for years, first of all with a friend and then on your own when he moved out of the city. He'd handed the tenancy over to you – an agreement that had somehow turned sour although you didn't go into details – and you'd quickly bought the flat off the council for a steal, your first step onto the property ladder. You'd lost contact with the friend, you said. He'd misunderstood the terms of the arrangement.

So when the council moved to buy the place back later on, at market value, you got all the money from the sale. A couple of hundred thousand – enough to fall out with somebody. You wanted to buy another place, but you knew it would take time. You were overwhelmed, you said. It was such a big decision. Of course, I offered to help. I always did.

We talked through your options, and the more we talked, the more an idea took shape in the spaces between our conversations. An unspoken suggestion. I could feel it growing, becoming more solid. Harder to ignore. But I kept my eyes away from it for a while, measuring it up, feeling the weight of it. I wasn't sure I was ready.

We were eating dinner at my place when we finally said it out loud. What if we moved in together? What about we buy a place: you put down the deposit and I do it up? We could design it just how we wanted it. A place for our future.

It felt right. Being in one place all the time, rather than sharing ourselves across two flats. Being a homeowner, something that had always felt out of reach to me. Being settled. Being with you. I wanted it. I wanted all of it.

We talked for a long time about how we might make it work. I was uncomfortable about the money. It was too uneven. You offered to make the whole of the downpayment, knowing I had nothing in reserve to contribute. But you reassured me. I'd do all the work. I'd find us a project, a doer-upper. You'd bring in the money, but I'd execute the design. So we made an agreement: I'd work out my teaching contract, and then I'd be a builder for a while. I had some experience; I'd helped a decorator friend out on a few odd jobs when money had been tight. And I could learn new skills. You had faith in me. We'd be a dream team. I was so good with my hands...

I was seduced all over again. I could never say no to you.

By the time we'd settled on a plan, the end of the year had arrived. We spent our first Christmas together at your place. You loved the holidays. It was all about family, you said. Following traditions, and making new ones of our own. I'd never really been a fan, so I was happy to just make you happy. We'd have your parents over. I would visit my family the week before, and try to ignore my mum's disappointment. A pattern set, so early on.

You were like a kid, decking the house out, delighting in hanging lights in every room. We bought a neon reindeer and suspended it in the window. You said it was our first tradition. One just for us. The first of many to come.

I spent every penny I had on a shiny red blender. A KitchenAid. The ultimate middle-class status symbol. Ironic, since you professed to despise the bourgeoisie. I offset the panic I felt when

I paid for it with the anticipation of seeing your face when you opened it. We had Christmas Eve on our own, so I gave it to you then, watching as you unwrapped it and then falling back on the sofa as you unwrapped me. You made everything feel magical and exciting; how Christmas was supposed to be. I almost changed my mind about it all.

Almost. Christmas Day itself was different. Your parents and your sister arrived, and suddenly everything was too loud, too stressful. Your father sat in a chair banging his walking stick on the floor, rapping out a maddening staccato that set my teeth on edge. Your sister and her children spread out across the flat, while her husband sank into the sofa drinking can after can of beer, popping ring pulls with a quiet determination. Your mum hovered in the kitchen, fussing over the vegetables, making you feel under scrutiny, undermined. You chose the menu, chose the timings, chose the music. You wanted everything to be perfect, but I didn't understand what perfection looked like. You hadn't shared your vision with me so instead I was a spare part in this rehearsed routine, repeated over decades, impossible to insert myself into. I retreated to our bedroom mid-morning to call my parents, and felt foolishly alone, out of place. I was surplus to requirements, wanting only you to myself.

It annoyed you, my feeling outside of things. You said I was being needy. You didn't understand how overwhelming it was. The noise and the arguments and the taking over of our space. Your space. I didn't know where to put myself in it when they were all there.

I kept making excuses to get away. I made calls from the garden, I went to pick up mint sauce from the corner shop. Then I hid in the kitchen, prepping and stirring and chopping. I thought I'd come up with a workable solution.

But you didn't like it. You said they were my family now, as well as yours; I ought to be in among them. I tried to explain, to say I just needed a bit of a breather. That I missed my people. That I felt a bit sad. Christmas usually did that to me. I was OK in the kitchen for now. I was happier with a bit of room to myself.

I tried to kiss you, but you pulled away. You were angry. You wanted everything to be perfect and I was ruining it. Why couldn't I get into the spirit, like everyone else? Why did it all have to be about me?

I was hurt. You didn't get it and you didn't care. You couldn't see things from my perspective at all. I said all of that to you, and could see you were unmoved. Your frustration grew, and all of a sudden we were hissing at one another across the kitchen table, keeping our voices down so your family didn't hear. We became heated, vicious. And then, madly, you picked up the knife I'd been slicing carrots with, lifted it to shoulder-height and tossed it sideways at me. I couldn't believe it. The knife hit the side of the cupboard behind me and fell to the floor as your mother walked into the room. I moved my gaze from the floor to her face, fixing my own with a smile and saying I was just popping out to the loo.

I walked past you without looking your way, and slipped into the bathroom. I needed a minute. You threw a knife at me! How mad was that? I knew it was an act of frustration rather than murderous intent, but still. What the fuck was I supposed to do about that?

I sat on the side of the bath. I could already hear myself telling the story to friends. 'Yes, I had a lovely Christmas thanks. I got some new pyjamas, and my girlfriend threw a knife at me.' Of course I'd play it for laughs. It was too bleak to portray it any other way. Besides, it *was* kind of funny. Part of me always enjoyed the sheer drama of your baddest behaviours.

After a few minutes, I headed back to the kitchen where I was relieved to find you alone. You came over to me and slipped your hands around my waist. Let's not fight, you said, I just want us all to have a lovely day together. It means so much to me. I kissed the top of your head, and promised we would. I didn't notice you hadn't said sorry. I was just glad it was over.

You moved into my place early in the new year, after the sale of your flat had completed. Most of your belongings went into storage. I

8

helped you box them up and move everything in a hired van to one of those soulless concrete hangars just behind the flyover.

And then we lived together. Just like that. It was wonderful, actually. We'd got over the Christmas blip – we never spoke about it – and we were back in our bubble. And in an interesting time and place. My street was being rapidly gentrified by the 'creatives' and trustafarians overrunning the borough. We saw them at the weekends giving guided tours of the neighbourhood to parents who'd bought them their little 'starter' flats, cash purchases. They all took the same route, touring past the Turkish shops and the new juice bar and the one decent café, down to the River Lea and on to the marshes beyond. We slagged them off while delighting in the delis and bars that began to muscle their way in between the chicken shops and pound stores on the streets around us. We bought sourdough and coffee at the weekends and good French wine in the week, and we settled into our shared space like we were on holiday: every day was an adventure. We were both on our best behaviour.

I started house-hunting for us. We talked about where we wanted to live and agreed we were rooted in the borough. We loved it there, hipster invasion and all. The challenge was to find somewhere with potential, before they did.

I loaded all the housing apps onto my phone, made appointments with all the agents. I met Andreas in his Ray-Bans and Michelle in her branded Mini Cooper, and laid out our plans to them. We wanted somewhere in need of work. Somewhere with a garden. Somewhere with space for us to grow.

I had never felt more grown up.

We ramped things up further by getting a kitten. Tiny Rambo joined us one wintry night and we became sleep-deprived parents to a mad ball of ginger fur. I got to the end of my second term of full-time teaching, and started to look forward to an end of marking and lesson planning. I browsed, half-heartedly, for other teaching posts but found few, and was secretly pleased. I reassured myself that I'd be fine to pause my career for a while. Calling it a career at that point was something of a stretch anyway.

I saw a dizzying number of overpriced places, traipsing in and out of tiny houses with enormous price tags, marvelling at the brazen lies Andreas and Michelle and the others could spin out with straight faces. This one's got brilliant storage, as I was shown a cupboard bolted under a staircase. This one has outdoor space, as I hung over a windowsill to view a cement rectangle below.

I remained optimistic. My sunny disposition never faltered. I knew we'd get somewhere amazing, because we were amazing. We were meant to be. And so was our house.

And then one day I found it: a damp, damaged flat on the top two floors of a Victorian house and a share of the garden below, with a bankrupt landlord and plant life growing out of the walls.

It was perfect.

I took you to see it, and talked you through where the walls could be knocked down, where doors and windows would be punched out. I was so sure of my grand plan. And you said yes, you were sure too. I loved it that you had faith in me to do it.

It took months to actually buy it, after untangling the mess of management companies and holding agents that had been put between the building and its corrupt owner. Stacks of unpaid bills were piled on the doormat when we went back to look again. The flat below was to be sold too, but in the meantime it would lie empty, leaving us to make as much noise as we liked with our renovations. And anything else.

I found a builder who would help do the work I couldn't. Nikolai had a gold front tooth, a bone-crushing handshake and an unmistakable air of menace. I liked him straight away. I tailed him round the flat as I spelled out what I wanted doing, hesitant at first, looking to him for approval. This is not a problem, he said, over and over. I was bolstered by his confidence, grinning like an idiot. He liked all of my ideas. I liked him even more.

By now it was April again, and we celebrated our first anniversary. We went to the river as we had done on our first date, more relaxed in each other's company than a year before. But still attentive, still desirous. Still so happy to be together. It struck me how much of my life had changed in twelve months. My work, my home, my friendships: all had shifted. You were now at the centre of everything.

That year we had another summer of fun, with plenty of evenings spent outdoors drinking and eating, with or without the company of others. We'd settled back into our friendship group as a couple, everyone now used to us being together, old affiliations remoulded to the new shape we took up. You had met and made friends with my oldest mates and I had learned how to get along with your family, found a space for myself in it. Everything seemed to slot so easily into place.

The nights began to draw in, and my teaching contract came to an end as the purchase of the flat finally concluded. It was time for us to make the move to our new lives. Joint homeowners, common-law spouses.

I was sorry to leave my flat – my first and only place of my own – but I was raring to go too. We spent our last night there holed up in the living room drinking wine and listening to music as I packed up the last of my things. The downstairs neighbours put their heads around the door to say goodbye. The ones we listened to most Sunday mornings as they shagged away their hangovers. We giggled as they left, remembering it. We'd miss them.

The next day was grey and miserable. We picked up coffees, and drove over to the new flat, pulling up outside as the rain started to pour. We'd forgotten all of its flaws, four months after I'd first found it. We were deflated by how grim it looked. Once inside, it was freezing cold, full of damp and there was dust and dirt everywhere. But you were wonderful; you set up the kitchen with our bits and pieces while I hauled furniture out of the van, and by the afternoon we had everything piled in and covered up, and a mattress on the floor in a room upstairs. We ate lunch at a makeshift table – a stack of two cardboard boxes full of my books – and made plans for managing the chaotic few weeks ahead. Nikolai and his team were arriving on Monday and from then until well into the new year, we'd be living in a building site.

When I think back on those months now, I can't recall the mess and the disruption. I only remember how exciting it was. And how intimidated I was by the Russians. I worked alongside them for the first three months of the renovations, trying not to look like I was completely out of my depth. They got on with ripping out pipework and smashing down walls. I tidied up, and took out the rubbish. 'You should wear gloves,' one of them said to me. 'Your hands look very soft.'

You would come home in the evenings and I'd tell you about our progress that day. You spent hours on my Mac poring over paint colours and obsessing about light switches and plug sockets. You said it was the details that would make the flat perfect. I said it was buying what we could afford that would make the flat finished.

Money was really tight. I took on freelance work, copyediting dull academic texts, working late into the evening after a day on the renovations. Sometimes I'd have to go into an office, and I'd revel in the warmth and comfort of the bland, beige building, swivelling on my chair with a coffee and being grateful for sitting down. We paid the Russians in cash for everything, so I'd withdraw wads of money on my way home and worry about being mugged. I worried about a lot of things. I worried that we couldn't afford materials, that the Russians would misinterpret my directions, that I would fuck up something fundamental. That I'd let you down. I was always so worried I would let you down.

One morning I left for work before you did, leaving you instructions to pass onto the Russians about where to cut a recess into a wall. I wanted to fit part of the kitchen into it, and Nikolai agreed to help me get the opening ready. You got the measurements completely wrong, so that when I got back that night Nikolai was waiting, flustered. 'This not right, no?' No, it really wasn't. The hole he'd left behind was twice what it needed to be, but he'd followed your directions. It wasn't his fault, as he was quick to point out. And it was reparable; I'd just have to re-lay the bricks he'd torn away. You got home just as we were figuring all of it out, and knew straight away what you'd done. You burst out laughing. And it made Nikolai and I laugh too. He thought you were such a ditz after that; it became a running joke that you weren't allowed anywhere near a tape measure. I was just so relieved it was your mistake, not mine. I knew it wouldn't have been as funny the other way around.

That Christmas, we decamped to your sister's house and we watched her and her husband play out the muted bickering and furious whispering that I now recognised as part of your family's festive tradition. I admit it was fun. We then spent New Year down in Brighton with our friends, a whole bunch of us split across different houses. Half the group, including us, was crowded into a too-small two-up two-down terrace, where we were allocated a blow-up mattress in the front room. The door to the street opened straight onto us, and our room was also the thoroughfare between the kitchen at the back and the bedrooms upstairs.

I was frustrated by the lack of privacy the first night. I was knackered, and my body ached all the time. I wanted to sleep more than anything else, but we had to wait until everyone else had gone to bed before we could finally lie down. In the morning, on New Year's Eve, we were up as soon as the first person came downstairs, tiptoeing loudly past our heads to put the coffee on.

I didn't realise it was annoying you as much as me. But that night, we saw the new year in with the others and then left the party early, sneaking back to our mattress and undressing one another impatiently, rushing to be naked before anyone else got home. It was freezing cold in that room. But you insisted I take everything off; you wanted to see all of me, feel me against the length of your own naked body. I can remember steam coming off your skin when we lay back sweatily later on, throwing off the covers to cool down. I had only just hit the lamp off when the door opened and everyone tramped in. We pretended to be asleep. I could feel you smiling against my chest.

The start of the year was hard work. It was always cold in the flat, and there was so much to do. January was a slog and I often wondered whether I'd made a mistake. Whether I could do what I'd promised.

When the Russians left in February, I was on my own. But I didn't panic. I learned new skills, figuring out how to tile walls and strip floors so they were finished neatly, looked professionally done. I hung doors, I built shelves. I fitted a kitchen. I spent two days with a hammer and chisel knocking plaster off brick, revealing a fireplace and hearth, lugging bag after bag of rubble downstairs and off to the tip. I was proud of myself. You said, often, you were proud of me too.

We more or less got the upstairs sorted as spring arrived, but we were still living like campers inside a brick tent. Without proper plumbing, we washed our dishes in the bath every night, filling the kettle from the bathroom sink. We held a mini celebration when the kitchen tap finally went in, toasting the running water with red wine. A small miracle, after weeks of hard graft.

Slowly, things were finished. I started to relax. I hadn't known I would be able to do this work – I'd bluffed to you that I could, that I was confident – but I'd figured it out along the way. A few things got fucked up, but never anything I couldn't fix or do again. And it was worth the pain and the stress when I saw your appreciation of what I'd done. You'd boast about it when we met with friends, stroking my ego as well as my leg while they looked on amused. It distracted me from the rips in my skin and the bruises on my body. It was absolutely worth it.

It took a full year to finish everything, and even then the next twelve months threw up new jobs all the time. There was stuff we could only afford as time went by. But I'd done it: I'd created a home for us, and we were happy. I felt so lucky to have it, and to have you. I'd never dared dream I'd have so much.

We celebrated another anniversary that spring, this time staying home and having dinner outside. I set up a table and chairs in our garden, a first, and we ate dinner and felt self-conscious about the neighbours. No one else used their gardens on our street. We were the middle-class wankers that did that kind of thing.

I went back to teaching in the autumn, finding another crappy placement on a temporary contract, but relieved to have something to move on to. And life got into a routine of work and weekends away or hanging out around the neighbourhood and seeing friends. I was content. I thought you were, too.

There were blips. We had a spectacular falling-out over getting a cleaner – a statement I never thought I'd make. The argument ran for weeks before coming to a head one Friday night when we'd both had too much to drink. It was mad. I still can't quite believe what happened.

I didn't want to get a cleaner. I was deeply uncomfortable with the idea of having a woman in our house cleaning up after us. I told you this. I explained that I didn't want to hold up the system of shit-work. I didn't think it was right: cash in hand, no sick pay, no holiday pay, no job security. You said that you'd find us a male cleaner. I said that wasn't really the point, but that if you could, I would agree to it. I was confused by your arguments. I got hustled.

But guess what? You couldn't find a man to clean our house. So you said you'd find a cleaning company that employed its workers ethically, gave them contracts so they got benefits and a decent salary. I said go for it. But you couldn't sort that out, either. Go figure.

So you lied. You told me that the lovely Hungarian woman who started working for us was permanently employed, part of a progressive company that looked out for its staff. You told me to get over my middle-class discomfort about cleaning, that it was me who had the problem, who saw such work as demeaning or devalued. You told me you'd sorted it.

And then one night when you were pissed, you told me I was an idiot for believing you about it all. That we were paying the Hungarian a tenner an hour cash in hand, and she could do what she wanted with it. It wasn't for us to make choices for people in that way.

I couldn't believe it. I asked if you were serious. I asked why you'd lied. It felt as if you'd actually cheated on me.

You were unrepentant. You said I'd made way too big a deal of it, that I took myself too seriously. Your mum had been a cleaner, there was nothing wrong with it as a job. I was a snob.

That's not true, I had protested. It wasn't about that. It wasn't about making choices for or about people, you'd distorted what I'd said. I ended up feeling like I was in the wrong, that I'd behaved badly. I was learning that this was a skill of yours: twisting reality so that you elicited apologies rather than offered them. I went to bed that night feeling confused and miserable, and couldn't shake the uneasy feeling for days after. In the end, I decided just to bury it. Everything else was good, it was just a stupid misunderstanding. Let it go.

I should have known then. I should have seen you more clearly. I should have been better prepared.

We'd talked about getting married for a long time. I'd waited three whole weeks after first kissing you before telling you I loved you, and I wanted to marry you, and I wanted us to have children.

16

I'm cool like that.

But you'd smiled and asked me to say it again, and said you wanted that too. So it had always been on the cards. Now and then it
came up and we wondered if we'd ever do it.

Then one day I decided we should. Looking back now, I know
that decision was partly based on an unease. I didn't feel safe. The
flat was in both our names but you'd put the money down for it. If
we broke up, wouldn't you just kick me out? Somewhere in the back
of my mind the story you'd told about how you acquired the tenancy
for your last flat lingered. I must have known, deep down, that you'd
done something wrong. And you could do it again.

But I also wanted the wedding. I wanted what other people had:
the validation and the celebration of who and what we were. I was in
love with you. I wanted a day where we stood in front of our friends
and family and I said that to you. It felt important.

So I proposed again, properly this time. I woke you up one weekend
morning with coffee and a pendant I'd found for you in a jeweller's
in Soho. Not a ring; I knew you wouldn't like that. Too traditional.
Too straight.

I'd had the necklace engraved with our initials, and I watched as
you opened it, and looked at me quizzically. It's not my birthday?

No, I said. This is for something else. I thought it was time I asked
you properly. Will you marry me?

I was so relieved when you smiled.

You ran with the idea straight away. You had big plans. We decided on
an afternoon wedding followed by a party at a place by the river, looking out onto the water. I didn't want anyone to have to pay for a thing,
so we'd have to find ways of providing all the food, all the drink, all
night. No problem, I said. We'd have to save, we'd have to wait. We'd
have to do some of the work ourselves. I knew that it would be me
putting in the hours. I didn't mind. I was excited about it.

It became another project. I had to manage budgets and orders and – the hardest part – expectations. I hated the disappointed look on your face when something was costed up at way more than we could afford. As outgoings racked up, I did something I'd never done before: I asked my parents for money. I was surprised they were happy to make a contribution. I hadn't considered this would be something they'd enjoy getting behind. They were pleased I was including them. I was touched they wanted to be included.

We booked in the date: four years to the day since we'd spent our first night together. It was a long build-up, more than a year of planning. I organised the venues, the food, the photographer, the barbecue, the barman, the backline for the band, the DJs. I sourced biodegradable plates and cutlery, built palm tree props for the beach theme you wanted, drove to France to stock up on cheap champagne. I became a semi-professional party planner. It could always be a fall-back if the teaching fell through.

You spent months scouring the internet for the perfect outfit. I told you to spend whatever it took to get something you loved. You found it eventually, a sleeveless jumpsuit that made my heart jump when I saw you in it. And you found me a white suit that made me look sharp, and cooler than I am. We were ready.

We had to give our notices at Hackney Town Hall three months ahead of the big day. We waited in line with other couples before we were called, separately, into side rooms to sign our paperwork. They checked we weren't marrying for practical reasons: no, I said. This one's for real.

Did you mean to marry me? Did you understand the vows that we took? Did you just want a day with you at its centre? I don't know the answers to these questions, now. I don't understand why you did it.

It was raining when we woke up on the morning we were to marry. What would Thomas Hardy say about that? But I was undeterred, confident the sun would come out later. It did, actually.

The flat was full of your family, shouting and fussing and making me feel stressed. I went for a run to get away, and to get rid of some of the adrenalin coursing through me. I wondered if it was OK to have a drink at 11 a.m.

In the end, there wasn't time. I went across to the hotel where my family were staying and felt calmer in their company. By lunchtime, you and I had decamped to the hotel where we'd spend our first night as newly-weds, and took our time to get dressed and ready. Your sister arrived along with my best friend. The four of us drank champagne and tried not to get too giddy. And then suddenly we were in a cab and heading to the town hall and everyone was there and they were all in their best party outfits and they were looking at us and a man called Vaughan was taking our photo. We went inside and took our seats at the front. I stumbled over every line of my vows while you squeezed my hand and smiled at me. And then we were married. Just like that.

It was a relief when it was over. I hadn't anticipated feeling that nervous, that exposed in front of everyone we knew. It was somehow too revealing. So I was glad to get out onto the town hall steps where I could crack jokes with my friends while the photographer corralled us into a group and made us shout cheese.

Photos done, we boarded a bus that we'd hired to take everyone to the wedding party. It was meant to be a highlight of the afternoon – and it was, in the end, but for reasons we hadn't anticipated.

The driver had never driven anything bigger than a transit before. He made many valiant attempts to manoeuvre the bus onto the main road but he got the turning angles wrong every time. I think he panicked. I felt for him. I knew what it was to feel the weight of expectation hang heavy on your shoulders.

It didn't look like we would be going anywhere. Another ten minutes later, and we noticed that two homeless men had got involved. It was them that helped direct the driver out of the tight curve of the town hall drive and onto the highway, at last. There were cheers from passers-by as well as our guests. The photographer loved it, telling us it was part of the day we'd want to remember. Sure enough, shots of the two homeless men made it into our wedding album. The one I burned to a crisp two and a half years later.

It was a good wedding. Everyone said so. We left for our hotel in the small hours, but our friends carried on the party all night. For once, I wasn't sad to miss it. We were so tired when we got to our room that we barely spoke before we fell asleep in the huge white bed. In the morning, you were grumpy, and hungover, but I insisted we stay there just a bit longer, before going back home to see everyone. I wanted you to myself. I wanted to consummate our union, as I kept saying to you with a grin. You didn't find it funny.

We began to talk about becoming a family. I had always wanted to have children, and I finally felt I was in a place – in a relationship – where it could be possible. You said you wanted it too, and we thought about timelines and money and space, and how and when we could make it happen. At first you seemed as enthusiastic as I did. But slowly it became a thing on the backburner. A future plan. A maybe, not a definitely.

I felt the hurt of it, but I was busy, too. And I was happy in my life. Our life. I was teaching full time again, and being commissioned to write too. I finally felt like I was getting somewhere. The flat was finished, and we were in a great part of town with friends nearby. I felt lucky. It seemed churlish to keep bringing up the one thing that I didn't have.

I wonder now if it was this that drove you away. I watched you with our friends' kids sometimes, and I was always aware of your distance from them. You never really engaged. I would clown about and throw myself into whatever game they wanted to play but you would smile and quickly disentangle yourself, slipping away to sit with the adults while I played entertainer. I didn't put too much store in it then: it was perfectly reasonable to prefer the company of grown-ups, after all. But while I loved seeing our friends' children, and my nephews and nieces, you were always aloof around them. I think it annoyed you, sometimes, that I had so much fun with them. You'd make snide comments about my boundaries. You'd remind me they weren't *my* children. I didn't need to go on about how wonderful they were quite so much.

You got a promotion at work, which meant you officially put talk of children on hold. For now, you said. You needed to bed in to your new job, show your team how good a manager you were. You needed to focus on you for a while.

Sure, I said. We have all the time in the world. Not strictly true, but I had faith we'd get back to our plans in time. This was far too big a thing for me – for both of us – to simply shelve. I'd just have to wait, that was all.

But then slowly, almost imperceptibly, things started to change. Looking back on it now, it was like the sunlight went out of things. Did you feel that too? Or was it you that was drawing the blinds across, casting a shadow over what we had made? Did you decide then you wanted out? Why didn't you tell me?

We began to argue much more often. You'd get annoyed about the smallest things, accusing me of not putting you first if I met up with friends or stayed later at work. You'd confuse me by saying it was fine if I did something for myself – a day out with friends or even just a long run – and then calling me repeatedly to see what time I'd be home. It was like a test that I couldn't work out the formula for, let alone the solution: I was bound to fail.

You said more and more often that you were glad it was just the two of us. You talked about travelling, a long trip to see the world, or about moving to the coast to be nearer to your mum. I was unsettled:

I loved our flat and hadn't considered leaving it, or leaving London. I didn't want to. I didn't understand why you did.

I invited you to a work event, a big-deal public-facing launch where I'd been asked to speak about my work and present some of my ideas. My career was beginning to take off and I was so glad to be part of a team again. You phoned me minutes before I was due to talk, saying you were lost, could I come out to find you. You were furious when I said I couldn't, that I was literally about to take to the stage. I started my presentation flustered and upset, and was distracted even further by your arrival midway through, whispering loud apologies as you elbowed your way into the room. It felt like you were trying to undermine me, but when I said that to you, you hit the roof. Not everything was about me. You'd been really upset to have been so late. I was an arsehole for making you feel worse.

I played the role of happy spouse when we were in the company of friends or family, but things were uneasy between us. I became insecure, wondering if you had started to go off me. I was more tentative, less sure of myself. I was needier. You were right about that. I hated it.

And you knew it. You held yourself away from me at home, going to bed early and getting up even earlier, crowding out intimacy with your routine of yoga and swimming and reading alone. You would keep your distance from me when we went out in a group, so that I'd have to seek you out when I wanted to leave, asking for your permission, for your company. You started to say no. I think you took pleasure in it, this new way of controlling me. Keeping me at arm's length so that I was always chasing, always ready to acquiesce to your wishes.

I should have spoken to someone about what was going wrong. I should have been less private, less proud. But I didn't tell anyone.

I hoped that we'd get back on track, slot back into the way we had always been. I didn't want anyone to think we weren't the perfect couple. I didn't want to shatter the illusion, even if the illusion existed only in my own head.

I grew close to a colleague, who jokingly referred to herself as my work wife. We would share lunches and long conversations over our desks, swapping opinions, finding much to agree on. I liked her a lot, but it hadn't crossed my mind that it was anything other than a friendship. You were frosty around her when we met you for a drink after work, seeing how close we had become. I was glad about it. It encouraged me to think we were just going through a rough patch. You still had feelings, you still wanted me. We'd be OK.

Out of the blue one night, the colleague leaned in and kissed me on the lips while we were standing at a bar waiting to order. The rest of our team were sitting across the other side of the room, and I remember being worried that they'd seen us. Then worried about you. I never worried that anything would come of it. It was unthinkable that I would cheat on you. It hadn't occurred to me in all the time we'd been together that I could want to be with anyone else. I couldn't. From the moment I first had you, I had only ever wanted you.

I thought about telling you, but decided it wasn't worth it. I didn't like having this secret, but in unburdening myself of it I'd only upset you. I'd give you a reason to be angry with me. I didn't think you needed any more of them.

So I spoke to the colleague over lunch the following week. She said she was really sorry, she knew about you, but she had just acted on feeling. I blushed, and told her nothing could ever happen. She heard me out as I talked about us, and how much I valued our marriage, even though it wasn't going well just now. She was really cool, nodding sympathetically and offering to stay out of my way if I wanted her to. We agreed to just forget the whole thing.

It shook me, though. It made me think about what would happen if you found out. Or if it had gone further. What then? Would I be happier if I fell into someone else's arms? Would I be doing it to make you take notice? Would you leave me? What would become of me without you?

It was an unbearable idea. I resolved to do everything I could to find what had gone missing between us, to relight our spark. I wanted to make you happy again. I wanted us to have fun, to see the light creep back across our marriage. We were having a hard time, sure, but it wasn't anything that I couldn't fix, if I just worked hard enough at it. I just had to make a plan, and keep trying.

After all, I would do anything to keep you. Anything at all.

Hendry, Price LLP, Family Law Practice: transcript of first consultation with Michelle Hendry, solicitor

Date of meeting: 31 October

By email

Thank you for coming in to your appointment with me today, it was a pleasure to meet you. I am very sorry to hear of the circumstances of your marriage. You confirmed in our meeting that you have been in a relationship with J for six years, married for two. You explained that the relationship has broken down, and that you are seeking to divorce J. I explained the grounds on which a divorce may be sought, and we went through each in detail. You said that you were worried that J would contest the divorce, or obstruct the process and that you would remain trapped in a marriage in which you were profoundly unhappy. I explained the process of divorce and went through a basic timeline for the dissolution of a marriage.

For the sake of clarity I have detailed the information we discussed regarding the divorce procedure, your finances and the catalogue of abusive and controlling behaviours you detailed to me regarding J. We arranged to meet again in a week by which time you will have told J of your intention to leave the marriage. I reminded you that no one can be compelled to remain in a relationship, especially one that is making them deeply unhappy and in which they feel in danger.

I reminded you that if J shows violence towards you at any time, and in particular if you feel you are under threat, you must immediately call the police. You must not at any time compromise your emotional and physical safety, and must instead rely on the law to protect you.

I have received payment of £500 for our initial consultation and you agreed to put on file a further £5,000 in order to cover the costs of obtaining a divorce using our services, as well as to enable us to begin negotiations concerning your financial separation from J. I am pleased that you have come to us for help, and look forward to working to achieve a positive outcome for you to enable you to start a new, happier life.

Divorce

You explained that you had been given my details by a colleague, on disclosing to her that you were unhappy in your marriage and you felt unable to leave. Your colleague had been sympathetic, and also greatly concerned. You had set out to her some of the background of your relationship with J, including the 'whirlwind' courtship at its beginning, and feeling that you were railroaded from very early on into making decisions that suited J. You gave as an example the decision to move in to J's flat after only a few months of being together, where J was able to control all the financial decision-making as well as dictate things like décor and choices of fixtures and fittings.

You also said that you had disclosed to your colleague that you felt J was controlling. Your colleague had strongly recommended that you also contact a domestic abuse organisation to seek expert advice. You told her that you didn't feel that was necessary, in particular because you had decided to seek divorce proceedings and felt that this would be the best course of action by which to remove yourself from a very unhappy marriage.

You told me that you were seeking divorce on the grounds of unreasonable behaviour. We went through a number of those behaviours. I explained that the test of unreasonable behaviour is a subjective not an objective one, i.e. you need only give reasons why you can no longer live with J, not 'prove' that J's actions are in any way objectively intolerable. You gave me the following information for the statement of your case:

1. that J would become jealous if you showed attention to friends or family members and would view this as being excluded, which was not the case. J would become upset and angry on these occasions
2. that J was controlling of your home environment and dictated the ways in which you lived as a household, which greatly upset you
3. that J would make inappropriate comments about your mental health, belittling you in front of friends and family

I explained that the divorce petition would be submitted to court, and a copy sent to J who would then have to respond. I further explained that the divorce petition only dealt with the matter of your marriage contract; the more complicated matter would be the separation of your financial commitments with J.
You expressed your concerns that J would contest both the divorce and any attempt to split your financial assets. I explained that in terms of the divorce petition, and because of the subjectivity of the unreasonable behaviour clause, it was extremely unlikely that J would be successful in contesting the divorce. Any legal expert would advise against such an attempt. In terms of financial separation, we agreed to work towards an

amicable agreement with J, if possible, but to keep in reserve the option of more direct methods of negotiation including, as a last resort, going to court. I advised that court proceedings were very costly, but that we had an excellent team in-house who would be able to deal with all aspects of such work.

I explained that we would write to J in the first instance to set out the particulars of their unreasonable behaviour. We would seek to reach agreement on these before proceeding further, but in the event that J opposed the information on the petition, or ignored our correspondence, we would nonetheless go ahead with submitting the petition to court. It is possible that J could ignore the court forms that will be sent to your home for completion that would entail agreement to the divorce; even in this case, as long as you can prove J has been served with the necessary paperwork, we will be able to proceed to the next stage. The process of divorce brings a legal end to your marriage, and will in total take around six months to complete.

I explained to you that you could seek a share of the costs of petitioning for divorce from J. You told me you wished to make the process as expedient as possible, and did not think that J would respond positively to a request for costs. Your priority was to finalise proceedings with minimum interaction with J. Your primary wish is to be free from your relationship, and to move on with your life as quickly as possible.

When we write to J we will be clear that you do not seek to claim costs and will confirm that you are prepared to pay both the court fee and the costs of the proceedings provided that they go ahead on an undefended basis. If the proceedings are either defended or there is any delay in returning the relevant documents to the court we will reserve the right to seek costs. I advised you that you would be able to change your mind at a later date about the issue of costs. I further advised you that we could begin the process of petitioning for divorce as soon as you indicated you were ready for us to do so.

You agreed to begin proceedings immediately, and said that you would inform J in person of your plans the following week. You explained that you would not do so immediately as you were going away with J for the weekend with a group of friends and did not wish to ruin the event for everyone, which had been long in the planning. You would inform me by telephone when J had been made aware of your plans.

Finances

I explained to you that it is always better to try to reach a financial settlement by consent, as this saves both time and money. If possible, we will achieve this by negotiating with J either directly or through J's legal team, once one is appointed. You expressed concern that J would be unable to afford legal advice; we would always recommend that such advice is sought in these matters, which would be to J's benefit as well as to yours. We will remind J in our first correspondence to seek independent legal advice in respect of division of the matrimonial assets.

In order to begin this process, I explained to you that we must first understand exactly what those matrimonial assets are. This will be arrived at through the mutual disclosure of financial information via Form E. We would seek to reach an agreement with J over a division of these assets. Once this had been agreed, we would submit a consent order to court which would become legally binding at the final stage of your divorce.

You explained to me that you were keen to sell your flat – the family home – as soon as possible so that you could buy a new property in the area. You would be frightened to continue living with J once you had broken the news of your wish to separate, and therefore wanted to put the flat to market immediately. I reminded you that you could not be compelled to remain in a relationship that was making you deeply unhappy, as well as compromising your emotional, psychological and physical safety. If you are in fear for your safety at any point, you should contact me immediately or else, and as well, contact the police.

You told me you had already looked at potential properties for purchase. You said that you felt you would be entitled to a great deal more of the share of the family home than J as you had made the larger financial contribution throughout your marriage, having been the main 'breadwinner' for most of the period of your cohabitation.

I explained that since you have made a much larger contribution to the purchase of the matrimonial home, you will clearly need to secure most of the equity in the home when it goes to market. We will make this clear in our correspondence with J. Although the starting point for any financial settlement would always be a 50/50 split, this would be altered based on yours and J's respective needs and resources, and the contributions you have made over the course of your marriage. We will have the opportunity of discussing this in much more detail as things progress, and we receive disclosure of all the assets. We also need to understand the relative costs of the arrangements you hope to achieve once your marriage has been dissolved, in order that we ensure your standard of living is maintained.

You told me you had looked into the level of mortgage you would be able to achieve, and had received confirmation from two separate lenders of the borrowing you could raise. You expressed concern that J would be unable to raise any kind of mortgage, having been freelance for a number of years prior to taking on their most recent job. I explained that J's capacity for borrowing would not impact the division of matrimonial assets.

You explained that you wished to remain living in Dalston, east London, since you had a network of friends and family in the area and, in particular, your sister lived nearby. You were aware that the cost of property in the area was relatively high, but felt it imperative to remain within close distance of this support network, who had kept you safe during your abusive relationship with J. For this reason you had sourced properties in and around the E8 postcode.

For the same reason, you were anxious that J not seek to also move into a new property in the area. You were reassured that J's work attracted a lower salary than yours, which would impact on their capacity for borrowing, as discussed. I explained that the financial agreement would in part be settled on the basis of need, and it was clear that your need to remain in your current neighbourhood was greater, reliant as you will be on the support networks you've built up there as you rebuild and move on from your abusive relationship with J.

You told me that J works in south London, in the Elephant and Castle area. You had sourced the particulars of a number of properties around Walworth Road, close to J's place of work. You feel these would be appropriate kinds of properties for J following your separation. You have sourced a range of studio and one-bed properties that are priced reasonably and reflect the amount of money you have calculated will be made available to J via any mortgage they are able to raise and your expected division of the equity from the family home. You told me that J does not have familial links to the area in which you both currently live, and that it would be more convenient and expedient for J to live closer to work, since J's working day starts early and continues well into each evening. I thanked you for having done this work in advance, which will be very helpful in our negotiations with J.

I asked that you detail your monthly expenditure, including all bills and other costs associated with running the home you share with J. You told me that you weren't sure of the exact amounts as J had always controlled your finances, and although all expenditure went out of an account jointly held in both your names, you did not have online access to this account and so could not easily check what went in and out of it.

You told me that your preference would be for J to move immediately out of the family home, and for you to take over payment of the mortgage in its entirety, as well as all bills and maintenance. You wish for J to rent privately for the period during which your flat is marketed and sold, and while a financial settlement between you both is agreed. You are very concerned that J will not agree to such an arrangement.

I explained that it would be sensible for us to write to J immediately after you have told J of your intention to leave the marriage. We would inform J that you were starting divorce proceedings (these would already be under way) and that you wished to keep things as amicable as possible, in order to reach an agreement that suited you both.

J has a legal right to remain in the flat, which you are aware of. You explained that you expected J to be particularly difficult about leaving. We discussed a secondary option of sharing the use of the family home, so that you occupy it for one week, and J the next. You agreed that this was a next best option, after J moving out completely, as you no longer wish to spend any time in J's company. I told you that we could also offer this arrangement at some point during our correspondences with J.

Negotiating a financial settlement should be straightforward but costs will rise if J is obstructive to our proposals, as you fear. There are a number of options for arriving at a final agreement including arbitration or a round-table. You told me you were not open to mediation of any kind, including lawyer-assisted mediation, as you felt J would be able to manipulate you into agreeing to things you were not comfortable with, as that had been the pattern of your relationship. You wanted to ensure you left the marriage with a good settlement in order to establish yourself in a new life.

In terms of your living arrangements, should J continue to exhibit controlling and abusive behaviour, it may be appropriate for us to apply for an order that will exclude J from your jointly owned property. In addition we may apply for a non-molestation order to further protect you. I can discuss protection with you in more detail once you have had the opportunity to inform J of your decision to leave. We understand that receiving such news can be a trigger for violent or abusive behaviour and so I discussed with you your options for protecting yourself under such circumstances, including informing the police as soon as you feel threatened.

We will do all we can to ensure you are given the space and security to deal with your separation from J properly. It is very important that you do not compromise your future financial security by attempting to negotiate with J without our support. I am confident we will arrive at a division of your matrimonial assets that will enable you to settle into a happier new life. I look forward to doing this work for you.

Chronology of abuse

You will, following this meeting, submit to us your diary entries from the past six months. These set out a history of abusive and controlling behaviour from J. You told me that, in retrospect, there were always indications that J was controlling, but in the early days of your relationship you overlooked these signs as you wanted to make things work.

Along with your diaries, you have compiled a chronology of incidents dating back over the last four years of your relationship with J.

You told me that you made contact with a DV helpline around two years ago, when you and J had become involved in a row after a night out with friends. J had accused you of belittling behaviour, which you disputed. You had been jokingly referring to J's fatigue at the end of the working day, J having just started in a new job that was very demanding. There had been some amusement among your group of friends that J was now working such long hours and in such a highly competitive environment because previously J had mainly made a living through being self-employed, and carefully selecting which jobs to work and what hours to keep.

You didn't realise that J had been upset by this conversation until you both returned to your flat, when J began shouting aggressively at you and demanding an apology. You were shocked by J's response, and did not understand why an apology was owed. J became increasingly agitated and aggressive as your conversation continued. Both of you had consumed alcohol. You told J you were going to bed and were not willing to engage further in an argument, at which point J physically blocked you from leaving the living room and heading upstairs. You were frightened by J's persistence that you apologise and by being contained within the same room, when J was so visibly angry with you. J threw an item of furniture across the room at you, which upset you enormously. You eventually escaped the living room and locked yourself in the bathroom, where you used your phone to find the details of a local DV service. You called their helpline but it was out of hours. You stayed in the bathroom until you heard J go to bed, after which time you went to the spare room to sleep for the night. You found this incident very frightening, and also confusing. You did not want to consider yourself as being in an abusive relationship, and so the following morning you made a concerted effort to placate J and to smooth over the argument.

You explained to me that J was controlling in other ways, for example in regards to your finances and your personal data. Since you moved in together, J has always handled payment of bills, arranged your mortgage, overseen the booking and payment of holidays, and so on. You have very little control or say over the finances held by you and J as a couple. Although you and J have a joint account, you do not have access to this account. You have tried to raise this with J, but feel you have not been heard. You believe J controls all the finances as a way of also controlling you. You opened a separate savings account 18 months ago into which you deposit a proportion of your salary each month. You explained that you have not told J about this account, as you anticipate it would cause an argument. You also explained that you have a separate pension arrangement.

You told me that J has also, on many occasions, demanded access to your passwords and personal information, for example your email account password. You described one incident when you had changed your password, denying J access to your email, only for J to accuse you of conducting an affair with an ex-partner of yours. You said that J had previously used the password to access your email account and had read through a number of messages you had exchanged with your ex, now a good friend of

yours, in whom you had been confiding about your unhappiness
and your uncertainty about wishing your marriage to continue.
Upon reading these messages, J had confronted you at home
and shown great anger about your 'duplicity' and 'betrayal'. You
had felt cornered and very exposed, and were concerned that
J would also show anger or violence towards your friend. You
were appalled that J had invaded your privacy in this way, and
had said so. In reply, J had accused you of being a liar, being
deceitful and being manipulative. You were deeply hurt by this.
J had once again shown violence by kicking the furniture in the
living room, which caused you to walk out of the house. You
were frightened to remain in your flat while J was so angry. You
wished for J to calm down before you returned, and sent a text
message explaining this. In reply you received a string of abusive
messages. You chose to spend that night at your sister's house as
she lived nearby and you felt it safest to be with her. J continued
to send you abusive text messages throughout that evening and
into the following morning.

You told me that on another occasion, following an argument with
J, you had once again been frightened to stay at the flat for the
night. You explained that this had occurred after a day of conflict
with J, conducted via email, where you had argued about your
relationship with your family. You explained that J was hostile to
your mum and your sister, feeling that they 'smothered' you and
left too little room in your life for your relationship with J.

You had felt exhausted by the argument, and had wished for an
evening without being bullied by J. You had consequently left
work, and gone for a meal by yourself in a restaurant close to your
offices. From there you made a phone call to your sister where you
confided that you were reluctant to return to the flat. Your sister
had spoken to you about J's behaviour, and had told you that both

she and your mother were concerned for you, and had spoken with each other about their misgivings regarding your relationship with J. In her opinion, J was isolating you from your family: you made less and less effort to spend time with them, and the frequency of weekends spent either at your sister's house or at your mother's had noticeably declined in the last 12–18 months.

Your sister had also noted details about your behaviour and your home life that were of grave concern to her: namely, that you were quieter on the phone than in the past whenever you spoke to her from your home, and that there were no photographs of her family and/or your parents on the walls of the flat you shared with J. In the past, you had always placed photographs of your family around the homes you'd lived in. Your sister felt that this change signalled the extent of J's controlling behaviour, even to the décor and interiors of your flat. She also felt that J prioritised work over you, and she had witnessed many occasions when J had been late to, or even not shown up for, social events that you had organised. She had talked to you about this in the past, and you had told her that J's work was both a passion, and all-consuming, and you were supportive of J's professional ambitions. Your sister had noted that this support was not mutual, and in fact J was often very dismissive of your work and your commitment to your clients.

Following your phone conversation with your sister, you had attempted to communicate with J by text message, fearing that a spoken conversation would be too difficult. There followed an exchange of text messages. All of J's messages were abusive and/or threatening. J told you that you would not be able to get back into the family home when you returned: you would be locked out. You replied with a text message to say you were coming back, and would ask your sister to accompany you. In response J sent a message saying it would be 'pretty fucked up for her to witness you not being able to get into your flat' and recommended that you stay away. In the end, you decided to stay at your sister's house for the night, where you turned off your phone. In the morning, you spoke with J and agreed that you needed some time apart. Accordingly, you remained at your sister's for the weekend.

You also told me about an occasion where J had used physical violence around the family home following an argument about your plans for your most recent Christmas together. On this occasion you had been very frightened by J's actions, to the point where you had considered calling the police. You decided not to, because you were afraid you would not be believed, following an earlier incident when J had locked you out of the flat. The argument had begun when you had asked that you and J spend Christmas with your sister and mother, instead of a group of J's friends. You believe that Christmas is a time for family whereas J, who does not have the same kind of family support structure as you, would rather spend it with friends or, indeed, alone. J accused you of reneging on an earlier agreement that you do not recall making, to spend it with friends and not at home. You were upset by this: you had always planned on spending it with your family. You believe J's refusal to agree to your plans points to a pattern of behaviour by J intended to alienate you from your family, with whom you have always been very close: a closeness that you believe J is deeply threatened by.

J became increasingly agitated during the conversation, and was furious that you would not back down on your commitment to being with your family. At one point, J had slammed a door so hard that a picture on the wall beside it had fallen to the floor and smashed. The picture had been given to J by an ex-girlfriend. J had blamed you for provoking their anger to the point of violence, and for causing the damage to an item that they valued. J had then punched the wall where the picture had fallen from, which scared you a great deal. You were afraid J would also punch you. You locked yourself in the bathroom, and eventually moved to the spare bedroom where you spent the night.

You also set out a pattern of undermining and critical behaviour, which you told me had always been a feature of your relationship with J but had become markedly worse in the last two years, since your marriage. You said that J frequently mocked you for being disorganised, calling you chaotic and comparing your methods for organising your work and social life unfavourably to theirs. Specifically, you described how J frequently became angry when asked for confirmation of times and dates for things you had planned together, saying that you were incompetent for not remembering this information and so making you feel upset. You told me that J had forced you to share an 'iCal' calendar, which you did not want to do, in order that they could see what you were planning and with whom. The effect of this was twofold: to diminish your confidence, and to allow J to monitor your social life and the plans you made with other people. J was also critical of arrangements you made with people close to you, for example your sister, or friends with whom you had had close relationships prior to your marriage. The effect of this was to cause you to withdraw from making plans with other people as you felt this would upset J, and you have consequently felt increasingly isolated and alone.

You then told me that J habitually referred to your losing items such as keys, bank cards and purses in front of your friends in order to mock and undermine you. You felt this made you look stupid and you were very unhappy about being the butt of such 'jokes'. Indeed, you said that J had on more than one occasion said you yourself were a joke, and that other people thought so too. You felt diminished by this constant criticism, in particular because of how J made you look in the eyes of your friends and family members. This has been a source of great anxiety and upset for you. You further described a situation last year when you had your bike stolen, and J had reacted furiously, calling you idiotic and incompetent. J had refused to help you sort out a replacement bike with your insurance company, withholding information on the details of your policy and your insurance provider, and instead telling you to take better care of your things. J had also refused to accompany you to the local police station where you reported the theft. You had been deeply upset by this, in particular because you had been the victim of a crime.

You also told me that J's criticism focused on the contribution you made to your household. J frequently accused you of not carrying out housework and other tasks associated with running the family home. You felt this was deeply unfair, but in spite of this you had made the suggestion that you organise a cleaner, in order that J not feel responsible for cleaning the house. You did not wish to spend the time necessary to keep the house clean to J's standards, but were happy to engage a professional service to do this for you. J had been extremely dismissive of this plan, and had refused to pay for outside help. You felt this was done deliberately in order that the solution you had proffered be rejected, allowing J to continue to position you as unhelpful and non-contributory.

Finally, you told me that you felt constantly afraid of J's temper, and it was this that had driven you to end the relationship. You felt the cumulative effect of all the incidents you had described to me had been to diminish your sense of self, and to make you feel stupid, frightened and alone. You deeply regretted not leaving J at an earlier point in your marriage, as you could see now that you would be much happier alone. You were exhausted by the continuous arguments that now characterised your marriage, and had come to realise that J's behaviour amounted to abuse and coercive control. You felt that you had, to greater or lesser degrees, always experienced J's behaviour as emotionally, psychologically and physically abusive.

You said there might also be other incidents that would illustrate this, but you were unable to recall them at this time. I explained that we could, at any time, come back to this account and insert any additional examples of J's behaviour that you were able to remember. I thanked you for taking the time to go through what is clearly a very upsetting chronology, and reminded you that it will help you to have this history set out as we progress your divorce and financial settlement.

If there is any aspect of our meeting today that needs further explanation, or you wish to contact me at any time, please do not hesitate to get in touch.

December

I had taunted you so many times about just putting an end to all of it. The daily, vicious text message fights. The tension during meals out and trips to the pub when I knew you weren't speaking to me, but I had to pretend everything was fine so my friends never asked me about us. I had dared you to leave. You had made me miserable for so long. I had tried to call your bluff, and I'd become sure you couldn't do it. Then you left, just like that. And now you won't speak to me at all. Why didn't I do the ending? Why did I let you lay me this low?

I can't stop myself sending you messages. Pleading with you to stay. Pleading with you to just fucking reply. I despise myself for doing this. I feel a deep, deep despair that I am now utterly cut off from you. How can you do this to me? How can you go from sleeping next to someone every night to absolutely nothing? What the fuck is the matter with you?

I looked up the definition of psychopathy: an inability to show remorse or feel empathy, a tendency to lie often, the habit of manipulating and hurting others. I think you're psychopathic. I have seen you lie so often, I don't think you know when you're telling the truth any more. I have watched you play the victim with our friends and your family so many times, making me out to be the bad guy. Over and over and over. I have felt like a trapped animal, contained within the bars of your stories, your lies.

I am not the bad guy.

Why did I ever think you loved me? I knew you weren't capable. You'd never shown it to anyone else, not really. You always rushed through explanations of past relationships: the married one, the one you didn't love, the one who was really just a friend, was still a friend now. I was curious. How had a friendship become more, who had blurred the lines? Had you really fallen for them, or they for you? Was it you that pulled back? Had you always been able to turn your back when things got complicated, to withhold your affections?

It was impossible to know the truth about your past. Why did I think we'd have a future? I'm as stupid as you are cruel.

I hate myself for begging. I squirm as I remember your threat to leave in the summer. My pathetic begging. The shame of it. A snot-faced mess on the floor. Why did I do that? I'd found your diary and what you'd written about us. About me. Terrible, terrible things. And I was so angry with you. Again, I wanted to know why. Again, I asked what is fucking wrong with you. But again you'd turned the tables, made yourself the victim. I was outplayed. I shut up. You shut down. You had all the power.

Why did you put me through that when you had no intention to stay? You made me have therapy! What a joke. Those stupid fucking sessions with Miriam, the middle-aged bespectacled cliché of a thera-pist who made doey eyes as you wept and told tilted versions of stories that I recognised but didn't understand. Passing you tissues with a practised, sympathetic nod. Those quick glances at her watch, be-cause really she's heard all this shit before a thousand times and she's thinking about her dinner. Or supper. I bet she calls it supper.

I remember vividly one session – there weren't that many in all. Four? Five? – when you, sobbing, told her you were scared people would think I was like your dad. Your bullying, miserable shit of a dad. You said you'd spent your childhood being afraid of him, that he terrorised you and your sister, and that you had watched your whole life as he criticised your mum and put her down. Miriam smiled ruefully (while wondering if she should have chicken or something lighter to eat later) as you described how your mum's meals were never good enough: the soup was too hot, or not hot enough. The casserole was too salty, or too bland. The veg was too hard, or too soft. While never lifting a finger to help, not even when your mum burned her hand carrying in an oven dish, or she knocked over the gravy and scalded her lap. What a shit your dad was. A horrible, nasty man.

But you saw the good in him, you said. You were able to see the scared little boy who'd never been held, raised in a children's home and incapable of connecting, who'd grown into the man that had tried to be loving but held a rage inside him at the adults who'd let him down. And that rage came out at the ones he felt safest with, so he threatened you and your sister with clenched fists and dangled belt buckles. Only threatened. Never hit. He wasn't a monster. You understood that. You, who always understood what people were really like. Your special gift.

And you were scared people would think I was like him, you said. You felt sad when people saw me lose my temper, because you thought they would pity me in the same way as you pitied your poor, impotent, raging dad. You just wanted to hold me, you said, to say it was OK. I was OK. I was loved.

You fucking liar. I wasn't loved. And I wasn't anything like your dad. Did it make you feel good to imagine this damage in me? It wasn't real. I am not the emotional invalid you have always painted me to be. It is you that is damaged, and damaging. You have wrecked me. Scuppered. I am unsalvageable.

You used those sessions in Tufnell Park – where else?! – to unravel me bit by bit. I listened quietly, nodding when you looked at me, focusing on getting to the end of another hour. Ticking them off, these conditions that you'd set on us. Clamping shut my mouth so that the protests I felt rising in my chest didn't escape, and I could get to the end having navigated a safe path. A path back to us. I actually hoped these ridiculous hours in a beige attic room might work, might be the miracle that would fix our shattered marriage. And so

I'd said the right things, and nothing more. And I'd made you laugh, sometimes, by mimicking Miriam's delivery as we left her comfortable house and got in the car. I remember that magical conspiratorial togetherness I loved to share with you. An in-joke, a secret smile. Playing the fool. I must have looked ridiculous to you.

You walked out and never looked back, while I debased myself in front of my colleagues, friends and family. The front door closed behind you and I texted my two closest friends: 'she's divorcing me'. Three short words, and a very short wait for their replies. They didn't sound surprised, only scared.

For me, not of me, before you start.

I called my manager, and lost it on the phone. She was so kind, and told me to come to meet her in Camden, we could travel to the office together... or not. I don't know how I got there. It's strange how the details get lost; there are just the set pieces, set in time, set in my mind with all else faded to grey around them. I met her in a coffee shop and we sat outside in the November chill, so she could smoke and I could be apart from the other customers, living their ordinary, gentle lives. I explained that you'd gone, you'd already seen a solicitor and things were in motion. I couldn't answer any of her questions: when, why, how, what now. I didn't know any of the answers.

While we sat, my phone rang, a number I didn't recognise. I stood up to take the call, stepping away from the table. It was your new legal team. Checking that they had the right number for me, for future contact. With British politeness I said that they did, then hung up and laughed bitterly at myself, my eyes stinging and my hands shaking. It hit me again that you were really doing this. You were gone. And then I remembered something. I'd had a feeling, a deep-down kind of fear, that something was happening the previous Monday. I'd said goodbye to you in the morning, when you said you were heading out for a morning meeting with your colleagues. You don't work on Mondays – you made a point of preserving this day for yourself; you said your work was too taxing to do it full time. It wouldn't be fair to you or to your clients. So I remembered feeling suspicious: there was something in what you were saying, or how you were saying it, that I didn't believe.

You'd left the flat and I'd looked at my phone to track your route into town. I'd watched the blue dot that was you as it moved from road to rail and back to road, reappearing at Holborn and then suddenly vanishing somewhere near Red Lion Square. You'd turned off your phone. I felt a chill when I saw that. It came back to me outside the coffee shop, that deep-down dread feeling that I'd put aside. And now I knew. You'd gone to see a solicitor, then come home to me and made up a different version of your morning that I'd been glad, desperately glad, to hear.

I dropped my phone to the floor, looking disinterestedly at the damage I'd done to its screen. I slid my back down the glass front of the coffee shop, collapsing into myself, head in hands. I didn't care that people were staring, that my boss was pulling me up, onto my chair, gathering my phone and my body back up to the table, telling me everything would be OK.

I knew with absolute certainty she was wrong.

She told me that I should take the week away from the office. I didn't have teaching hours, I was on a research contract, I didn't need to be in. I could work at home, but only if I wanted to, if it would be a useful distraction. Or if not, that was fine too. I stared at her. I didn't know my boss well enough for this to feel anything other than humiliating. I had absolutely no idea what to say or do. I could not imagine a single thing beyond drinking the cup of coffee in front of me. Everything had fallen away.

My boss had to step in to instruct me, issuing stage directions with the help of my friends, whom she contacted via the smashed-up phone on the table between us. One of them came to the coffee shop to get me, my boss handing me over like an errant toddler, removed from playgroup for upsetting the other children.

It was Zed who collected me, took me home with them, gave me a sandwich and told me to eat it. I fell asleep on the sofa instead. I always respond like this when I'm scared, my system kicking in to render me unconscious, away from what is overwhelming me. When I woke up the sun was setting, and Nancy was there too. She'd left work early to join my support crew. They were whispering about me, knotted brows and lowered voices. I hated being observed as I was. I didn't want to be this version of me.

They agreed it was sufficiently late in the day to start drinking, and so we did. I told them what I knew, which wasn't much. You had a proxy now, a legal team through which I was to conduct the end of my marriage to you. You didn't want to meet, you didn't want to talk. The time for all that was over.

So I called you, again and again. They told me not to, and I shouted what would *you* do? They didn't know, so let me be. How could they know? They'd never been in this situation. No one I knew had. I had to hand it to you: you'd come up with the most excruciating method of extraction, a departure without any of the anaesthesia of 'we can still be friends' or even 'we can talk'. And then suddenly you answered, your voice at the end of the line sounding just like you, which I hadn't expected, and which made it worse, somehow.

I asked you why. I begged you to stop. I wondered what would happen next. You made no reply, only saying calmly – so very calmly – that your solicitor would be in touch to set everything out. I told you I'd heard from them already. I told you how angry that made me. You said that's why it was best you left it to them to speak with me. And then you said you were going to put the phone down. So I yelled, and threw my phone again. And then I punched the glass of Zed's living-room window, again and again, until someone took my wrist and pulled me away and then I cried and cried and cried.

The next day went by in a blur. I went back to work and sat silently behind my screen. My boss encouraged me to talk to my colleagues about what was happening, but I wasn't ready to take her advice. I stayed late, and returned to our empty flat where the cat looked forlorn and lonely. It was strangely helpful. I talked to him a great deal, asking when he thought you'd come back. Where you were. Whether he thought you'd speak to him on the phone, if not me.

He didn't think so.

I phoned you again and again, and texted, without reply. I phoned your sister. I phoned your work. I checked your Facebook. Nothing. Not anywhere. There was a wall of silence around you, expertly constructed. Eventually, I phoned your mum. It was an admission of defeat: if she knew, then all was lost. I dialled her number at home and waited as it rang, three, four times. Then suddenly, a voice. It was a shock, after so many unanswered calls to you. She sounded small, and old, and suddenly very unfamiliar.

I'd always liked your mum. I felt protective of her, so many miserable years spent living with your bastard of a dad. But I realised as she answered that anything I thought we'd shared was gone. You had told her you'd left me, and she had closed ranks with you in the blink of an eye. I was an idiot to think it would be any other way. My voice choked as I said hello, and then asked if she knew what was happening. Yes, dear, and I'm sorry but I can't do anything for you. It's a shame but there you are. You just need to move on I suppose.

I suppose. Why waste time feeling sad when six years of your life suddenly vanishes without a trace? Why show emotion of any kind when you can just shut it all down, and eventually feel nothing at all? You once told me that during his working life your dad was regularly kicked off jobs, or stormed out of them. You said you admired him for this; he was making a stand about the way he and his colleagues were treated. He was a man of principle. And I always thought, I wonder if your mum agreed, when she was worrying about feeding and clothing you all. I wondered if she was proud of his fits of pique, his heroic defence of the working man.

I realised on the phone to her that no one would ever have known. She had spent a lifetime suppressing her own feelings, and had taught you to do the same. Cut it off, shut it down, move on. Between your parents, you had been taught that love is a combination of selfishness and silence. What a way to grow up.

God forbid you ever become a parent.

Your mum ended the call quickly, and it hit me like a train that I'd never see her again. I lay down on the sofa and stared at the fireplace, allowing some happy memories to creep in: your mum half cut on sherry doing hopeless charades, and that time she set the toaster on fire with a violently inserted French stick. I thought back to our wedding day, when she sat beside you at the reception, making everyone laugh with her stories of your forgetfulness.

Suddenly, I felt sick to my stomach at the thought of all of you. Your fucking family, with its twisted version of what home life should be. We've got to stick together, you always said. What happened to that? Another lie. You'd been taught to look after number one, first and foremost, and fuck everyone else. Just like your dad.

I stood up and grabbed for my phone, dialling your number again. Again, you didn't answer. I felt a deep, deep rage at your heartlessness, and your cruelty. I wasn't going to stick to your timetable. Fuck you. Fuck you and your dysfunctional fucking family. Fuck your lawyer. Fuck your diktats. If you weren't going to reply to me, I was going to start taking matters into my own hands. And that would start with our house. If you were leaving me, then you wouldn't get to keep any of the things I had made for us. I wouldn't let you enjoy the fixtures and fittings of our life together if that life was over. I would act first, and I would make sure I took back control. I knew you'd hate that. You hated it when you weren't the one in control.

The following morning, I called the estate agent who had sold us our flat. She was pleased to hear from me; it had been a while since I'd last been in touch, when I'd enquired about the value we'd added by renovating it. That I'd added. I'd done every bit of the work, while you'd held up the process dithering over plug sockets and the casings on the smoke alarms. Typical of you to sweat the small stuff. Typical of you to leave the hard work to me.

I told the agent that we were selling up, and I'd like her to come round again to value the place. She was excited for us, assuming we were taking the money and sinking it into another investment. Maybe somewhere in the countryside this time? Maybe we were planning to expand the family, nudge nudge wink wink. I didn't say anything, just murmured a little, and coughed over the really awkward parts.

I didn't know when you were planning on coming back, so I wanted to act quickly to get the house on the market. For the first time in forty-eight hours I felt some energy, some purpose. It was exciting to imagine your face when you realised what I'd done, that you weren't calling all the shots. I asked the agent if she could come the next day to make her assessment, and she readily agreed. We talked about photography, and I said I could send her professional shots I'd had done when we'd toyed with the idea of putting the house on Airbnb. It would save time, which was great for her. It was even better for me.

I put the phone down and smiled to myself. I wasn't going to let you walk all over me. I thought about our home, and everything I'd put into it to make it the place you wanted it to be. To make it ours. I didn't realise, until then, that it meant so much to me. The first place I'd ever owned. I was proud of it. I'd loved it when friends had come round and cooed over the open space, complimenting me on my handiwork. I loved it even more when you put your arms around my waist and told them how great a builder I was, how good I was with my hands. A secret smile, a laugh at my blushing cheeks. I didn't want for a second to actually part with it, this safe haven I had built for us. But I knew you loved it too and I wanted to make this real for you. To show you that what you were doing would smash not just me and my life into pieces, but yours too. I didn't think you'd considered this, not then. I thought that you were being foolish, chaotic, your usual self. I didn't realise how wrong I was.

And so I met with the agent the next day, and followed her as she went from room to room, offering the same compliments as our friends, congratulating me on a job well done. I smiled rigidly, thanked her weakly. She completed her tour, and we sat briefly at the kitchen table while she laid it all out. We could market it for a huge sum, more than double what we paid for it. We could expect a quick sale, probably a cash buyer. We could attract both successful young couples – like us – but also families looking to buy. It was a buoyant market. Flats like ours were like gold dust. It would go like a hot cake. It would set us up nicely for whatever came next.

I nodded dumbly and sanctioned the next steps: a listing on their website, a glossy brochure, a board put up in the street outside. I put my name to all of it, scribbling away on sheet after sheet of thick logoed paper. She never even asked for your signature. Why would she, you'd never been part of our business in the past. I wondered how quickly it would get back to you, this news. I wasn't going to whisper a word of it; I wanted you to come home and see the For Sale sign up outside and feel something – just a tiny fraction – of the pain you'd caused me. I wanted you to feel the same panic, that rising sense of dread, that had sat in my chest since you'd left.

The agent went away, all smiles, dropping her neat briefcase and neater frame into a small silver sports car before whizzing off down the street. I heard from her later that afternoon, a warm reassurance that all was going ahead, our home should be on the market by the end of the week, and buyers booked in as soon as possible to have a look around it. She already had some people in mind, in fact, a lovely couple who'd been searching for their next dream home and she thought this could well be it. Wasn't that perfect timing? What luck, for everyone.

I heard from you that evening, a text message telling me you planned to return on Monday, by which time I should be gone. Instructing me to stay with friends, as it wasn't appropriate for us to be in the house together. You said you understood the strength of my feelings but could not condone my actions. That it was unacceptable for me to express myself as I had, that my messages showed you that there was nothing for us to talk about. You were clear that you would not engage in conversations like these.

I recognised the tight, composed tone of the message: the same way of communicating that had so enraged me over the past... how long was it? How many months had you been patronising me with language like this? Your pseudo-therapy speak, collected at training sessions and conferences, and refined through conversations with colleagues you sought to impress. If it hadn't been so annihilating, it would have been funny. I didn't feel like laughing this time. So I held tightly to my chest the image of you arriving back to a house now in limbo, a liminal space, neither yours nor mine: soon to be someone else's. I was glad I had acted with malice. I was proud of being callous. Perhaps it would finally earn me some respect from you.

The weekend arrived and I felt a new kind of panic at the empty days ahead. I'd got through the week by working early and late, declining kind offers of dinner or a bed. I wanted to be at home, to maintain some semblance of the life I'd had. To sleep in my own bed, even though you weren't in it. To imagine that you were.

I hadn't slept, though. I'd lain awake every night feeling desperate. Occasionally I'd drifted into a kind of unconsciousness, but would jerk awake, wide awake, well before dawn. I'd selected an epic box set and spent the silent, still early hours watching tales of rivalry and rape and foreign empires. I was immune to its violence and stupidity. It was enough that it told a tale, and I could follow it.

Hearing its theme tune still makes my blood run cold.

But the weekend offered new terrors. What would I do when I was on my own for two whole days? What had I done before? I couldn't remember, and now everyone had partners and children and lives centred on their other halves. Without mine, I was less than half: I was nothing.

I couldn't handle the idea of going out into the neighbourhood. Things I'd seen a thousand times before were now unbearable: couples strolling by on their way to a breakfast with friends, someone picking up supplies to make brunch back at home, another strolling from the corner shop with the weekend papers tucked under their arm. The slowed pace, the gentle hum of two days' break from work. Two days to spend with your lover, your loved ones. Two days for me to spend alone.

I stayed in bed, watching episode after episode. I considered having a drink, but decided that even for me, even then, it was too pathetic. I realised I was hungry, but could think of nothing I wanted to eat. So I stayed under the duvet, and I kept the curtains closed, and I did nothing.

Except check my phone. I'd replied to your last message and heard nothing back. You wouldn't allow my feelings in, I knew that, so I had tried a different tack, telling you over and over that I loved you in spite of the terrible pain you were causing me, the damage you were doing. I loved you even though you were treating me like a monster. I knew you felt you had to do that, I understood everything about you. I loved you even though you felt like you were in control right now, because I knew that deep down you didn't know what you were doing and I would be here, like I always had been, to take back the reins when you were tired.

That was the twisted thing: I couldn't stop worrying about how you were doing. I had spent six years taking care of you, protecting you, looking after your needs and your plans and your belongings. I was conditioned to putting all of that first, and I knew you'd be useless at it all without me. I wanted to help you. In spite of what you were doing to me, I wanted to make you feel better.

Early on Saturday evening, I got out of bed and cracked open a beer. It felt shameful, but it had an immediate effect on my mood, lifting it from abject to manageable. I ate some toast, and decided to read the rest of my messages, so far ignored while I obsessively checked for yours. Zed had sent seven, reminding me that it was a good friend's birthday party that night and I was going to go. No excuses. Zed would pick me up at eight and take me there in a cab, and everyone would be glad to see me. They were all so worried. It was all so sad. They all wanted to know I was OK.

I decided that it was a better option than staying in the flat on my own. I showered and dressed and waited on the sofa for eight o'clock to roll around. I was distracted, momentarily, by the shit that is on TV over the weekend, the family shows they air around teatime. A stark reminder of what I'd lost, the family we'd never be. Your leaving smashed me in the face again, and so I drank, steadily. And I waited.

Zed arrived and bundled me into the cab. We realised I was quite drunk. I didn't mind, although Zed looked a bit worried. When we got to the party, I couldn't get out of the car. A combination of fear, dread and alcohol suddenly made it impossible for me to move my legs, so I told Zed I'd take the cab back home.

No dice. I was hauled out, and we staggered across the street and up the stairs of some smart west London pub into its packed function room. I saw plenty of familiar faces, and took up a stool in the far corner, my back to the wall, Zed beside me. My human shield.

I don't think I actually said hello to the birthday girl. What a wanker. I kept to my stool, greeting friends who came over to hug me and replenish my drink. Here you go, mate, that will help.

It did, actually.

I told Zed that you'd sent me a missive, telling me to vacate the flat by Monday. Zed said that was probably a good idea. I felt betrayed, and said so, but Zed was clear: you can't see her right now; you're a mess and she's angry with you. Do what she says, and she'll calm down and then you can talk.

There's nothing more annoying than a reasonable friend. I didn't need it. I wanted to be unreasonable, to be devastated, to be furious. I said all that, which Zed took pretty well. Another friend came over and offered me a room at her place, which Zed accepted on my behalf. She lived just around the corner from our flat. I figured it was my best option; it felt safer than staying miles away. I could be in touching distance of you. I would be able to walk past our home and even if you wouldn't let me in, I'd know you were there. I would still be connected.

I drank another beer, and another. Eventually, I was allowed to leave, Zed calling me another cab and giving me strict instructions to go straight to bed when I got home. Good advice. I should have taken it.

Instead I staggered inside the front door, gripping a plastic bag full of bottles I'd bought from the shop at the end of the road where I'd asked the cab driver to drop me off. I sat in the dark, drinking one after the other, listening to songs that reminded me of you. What a cliché. What a relief, this altered state. What a fucking headache, the next day.

I did what I was told, and left the house on Monday morning with an overnight bag. I went to work, kept my head down, got through tasks and didn't remember a thing about it by the day's end. I travelled home, the usual route. I walked to our house, saw the lights on upstairs, imagined you walking around inside. It felt utterly surreal. I thought about why I wasn't allowed in. Your decision. I held my key in my hand, feeling some sense of power that I could use it. Could walk straight in and confront you. And in that moment I decided I'd had enough. I was sick of your decisions. I was going to put myself back in charge.

I put the key in the lock and turned it. But it would only go halfway. You'd turned the latch down on the other side. You'd guessed right, again. A now-familiar surge of rage and despair filled me, and I briefly considered kicking the door in. Making another scene. I just didn't have it in me, in the end. I was tired of being stared at, and I was tired of losing. I knew this was a losing plan. So I turned and walked away, and spent the next seven nights in the spare room of two kind, confused friends who tried to make sense with me of what you'd done. And failed.

We all failed.

*

The next Monday was my turn to be at home. Lucky me. After work I took the usual route towards Dalston, feeling pleased that I would be back in my den. I wanted to feel safe again, and even if you weren't in it, I knew the flat would help with that feeling. But I was worried, too. I didn't know what you would have done during your days behind that locked front door. Would you have moved my stuff out of our room, or worse, moved your stuff out? It's a terrible feeling, knowing someone has the power to uproot your belongings. It had been preoccupying me and now was the moment of truth.

I put my key in the lock and took a tiny bit of satisfaction from seeing it turn all the way round. Take it where you can get it, I thought. I went up the stairs from the entrance hall and was greeted by an ecstatic cat. Rambo wove between my legs, and for a moment I smiled as I reached down to stroke his ginger head. I walked on, into the living room, and stopped still. Fucking bitch. I couldn't fucking believe it.

In the middle of the room, beside the fireplace, was an eight-foot Christmas tree, fully decked with all the lights and ornaments we stored in the loft. That we'd collected together over the years, each one a special moment, a happy memory. The lights were switched off which I took to be some tiny nod to my feelings, rather than an environmental consideration. Was it? Did you realise, in some distant cell in the underdeveloped empathic part of your brain, that it was fucking nuts to deck the house out as if we were actually celebrating the holidays? Did you consider that I might find it a bit… insensitive? That Christmas really wasn't the 'vibe' at the moment.

I lost it.

I grabbed the tree by its trunk and dragged it out of the room and down the stairs, yanking plugs out of sockets as I went. Needles and decorations flew everywhere, satisfyingly. Some of them I crushed underfoot as I stamped my way out of the flat, and smashed the tree down onto the path outside. I must have looked mad. I certainly felt it. I went back inside and wrote 'Please take: no longer needed' on a piece of A4 paper with a black Sharpie in big, spiky letters. I returned, and stuck a branch of the tree through the paper, holding it in place. Plugs and wires trailed from it back to the front door, so I kicked these towards its base and slammed back into the house. I felt better. A little. I knew that tree would be gone in the morning.

Then I snatched down the remaining decorations and lights from around the living room and kitchen, stuffing them into a bin liner which I put out next to the tree. I scribbled another note: 'Take Me'. I pondered whether to simply stick it to my chest, but the thought didn't amuse me for long. I left it on the bag, and stalked back inside. My hands shook, but I felt a moment of bitter satisfaction in taking from you something I knew you loved so much.

The next day, the front path was clear, bar a scattering of needles. The tree had gone, to a nearby family or one of the junkies down the road. I didn't care which.

It was a tiny victory. Take them where you can get them.

I went through the house, then, from room to room. Surveying, assessing, checking. Obsessing. What had you moved, what was different? And I began to calm down, because nothing had changed. Your clothes hung next to mine in the wardrobe, were folded beside my own on the shelves. In the bathroom, some of your make-up and toiletries were missing – but I had expected that. It didn't frighten me.

I swept up the scattered pine needles and shards of glass that littered the floor and stairs, and I relaxed a little bit. Things would be fine, I told myself. You needed to do the tree thing to make the house feel homely, I reasoned. It was a good sign. You were keeping things normal, in your own way, and things would return to how they were. You just needed time.

I sat down on the sofa with the pile of mail you'd left for me on the kitchen table. Most of it was junk, but there was a thick white envelope addressed to me that looked important. I turned it over, and my heart started racing. It had the name and address of a lawyer's office written above the gummed fold. My hands shook, and I felt the edges of my vision darken. I opened the envelope and took out the headed sheet: a single piece of paper.

'We are writing in relation to the unhappy state of your marriage. Our client advises that regrettably the marriage is irretrievably broken down and she intends to file for divorce on the basis of your unreasonable behaviour.'

I stopped breathing.

'If we do not hear from you within the next 10 days in this regard we will issue divorce proceedings based on the facts cited. Our client does not seek to claim costs against you and confirms that she is prepared to pay both the court fee and the costs of the proceedings provided that they proceed on an undefended basis.'

What generosity! How much does it cost to divorce someone? How much would it cost to defend myself? Did I have to defend myself? Against what?

Against the three particulars of my unreasonable behaviour, so stupidly listed on the page. Three shitty excuses to absolve yourself of any responsibility for this car crash of your making.

'Our client notes that you have put the property you jointly own to market. She wishes to remain in the family home and is prepared to pay the mortgage and all outgoings on the property in order that you use your income to secure a rental property. She hopes that once you have left the home you will be able to agree on the sale of the property and division of the assets so that you can both move on with your respective lives.'

Move on. Move out. It hadn't fazed you one bit, my putting the flat up for sale. You'd wanted me to. It only expedited your exit. I'd looked forward gleefully to your finding out that our home was at threat, expecting you to pull back. To pull back to me. What a fucking idiot.

You wanted me out. I wasn't going to go, I knew that much. I wasn't going to go. This is my home. I am not going to go.

I remember the disbelief. You had done this to me by letter. You had become someone's client. You were going to take everything from me, because you had the money – and the venom – to do this through lawyers. You knew I had neither.

'You are advised to seek legal advice with regard to the contents of this letter and we would be grateful to hear from you or your solicitor within the next 14 days.'

Two weeks. A fortnight to sort out my response. What the fuck was I supposed to do in response to that?

I hated you. I really fucking hated you in that moment. I wanted to confront you, to demand answers. How dare you treat me like this? How dare you threaten my home, my space? My sense of self. I had been holding tight against the panic that sat, a heavy constant, in the pit of my stomach, but this letter... this impersonal, expensive intrusion into the misery of my existence... it made me lose my grip. The fear became overwhelming as I tried to look ahead to a future without you, and without every single thing we'd had together. It was too much.

So I did what any self-respecting thirty-nine-year-old would do: finally, I called my mum.

She didn't know what I was saying at first, couldn't make out the words as my voice became shrill and rapid. I was insensible.

My poor mum. We knew you were having some troubles, but we had no idea it had got this bad.

Neither had I, Mum, that's the maddest thing. I thought we were working things out, and I was putting everything into it. I can't believe what's happening. I don't know what to do.

Come home. We'll look after you.

It was the only thing I could do.

By the time I arrived at my parents' at the end of the week, I had developed a stutter. I was so overwhelmed by what you'd done that my body could no longer process the things my brain wanted it to say. Words came out in a jumble of tics and pauses, repetitions of syllables that I could see were painful to witness.

I managed to record a voice message onto Rambo's cat feeder – a stilted greeting that would activate when his food was dispensed – before abandoning him for the weekend. I crashed in like a juddering wreck on my parents' suburban calm, to be greeted by my mother's worried embrace, my father's breathtaking insensitivity. Bloody hell, what a year this is. Your mother crashed her car, you know? Now you're getting divorced, and Liverpool are top of the league.

I knew it was an attempt at a joke. It was the kind of humour I'd inherited from him. But it caused me physical pain to hear him so casually drop the d-word, helping move along what was happening to me from an idea into a reality. I didn't want that. I wasn't going to let it happen.

There were memories of you in every corner of my parents' house. I hadn't anticipated them, hadn't expected that you'd invaded their territory, got behind enemy lines. I went upstairs to drop my bag off, and remembered the first time I'd brought you here.

I had been so nervous. It was significant, my bringing you to meet them, of course it was. But I don't think you knew what it meant to me, to have you installed by my side for a family weekend. I had so often, in the past, been on my own. A bit of a worry, I knew, for parents who just desperately wanted their offspring settled. A bit of a misfit.

But, with you, I felt like I'd finally made it.

So I couldn't wait to tell my mum and dad about our plans for the future, the house, the joining together of our lives. My mum had seen the besotted look in my eye, and had asked if I was sure about taking so much on. I had laughed, turning away from her hesitation. I think she saw through you, even then.

But you had been charming, laughing at my dad's jokes, and being attentive to me so that they could see I was loved, I was wanted. I had been so proud: of you, of myself for finding you. We had sneaked in kisses as we moved between rooms, and I had gasped as you groped me, a grin on your face, as my mum stepped outside to check on dinner and just seconds before my dad returned from the bathroom to drop himself back down on to his spot on the sofa.

I'd shown you my old neighbourhood haunts, walking hand in hand with you around streets where as a teenager I'd imagined a lover like you. A love like ours. I felt bigger, more important, with you on my arm. I told you secrets about the dreams I'd had growing up there, the plans I'd always hoped to fulfil.

I thought all those dreams had come true.

That night, my mum listened quietly to my side of the story, and put me to bed early. Tucked in at 9 p.m. on Friday night in my old bed at home – I didn't think I could be any sadder. My sister arrived the next day, looking worried but trying to rally me. She bit back comments about you. I overheard her saying something to my parents about seeing this coming, but mostly they just sat together, sadly. They worried. They wanted to help. They were as helpless as me.

I sat up late that Saturday talking to my sister, trying to answer her questions about what had gone wrong, why you'd left. I couldn't, not really. I said you'd threatened to go before, but I thought we'd been working it out. I'd been doing everything you'd asked, including going to fucking therapy, even though I knew you were using it as a way to trap me into saying it was all my fault. Drawing on your supposed expertise in dealing with difficult pathologies, pathologising me, creating the monster you said I was.

My sister listened. She asked me what I had done that might make it my fault. And I was devastated. I felt the darkness at the side of my vision again, that she, too, was making me the problem. I suddenly realised that if she could ask me what I'd done wrong, others must be thinking the same. It was the first flash of insight into what was to come.

Don't be such a fucking Alan, I said, summoning the worst insult I could muster.

Alan. The cartoonish goon of so many parties we'd staggered through in our twenties. Trying his handsy luck with all the women, succeeding with none. Donning a variety of hats – baseball cap, fedora, pork pie – to disguise his bald fucking head. Honestly believing that they would make him in any way acceptable to look at. Arrogant cock Alan, whom we all despised.

Imagine being as big a cunt as Alan, I said to my sister. That's what you're being right now.

It made her laugh. And I remember I laughed too. Then: the kids will miss her, she said, which devastated me all over again. I knew it was true. I wondered if you'd even thought about my nephews and nieces, or would ever again. It was just like you to wreak so much havoc, without a backward glance.

I told her I'd put the house on the market.

Oh wow. That's really real. Are you sure you want to make big decisions like that?

No, I wasn't. I had meant it as a punishment for you, a shock to your system that would bring an end to all this. But I'd got it completely wrong, and shot myself in the foot instead. I told her about the lawyer's letter, and the terms you'd already set for leaving me. She was shocked, then, that you'd been so underhanded. So brutal. It was some comfort to me to see her react in the way I had. To see her start to shift her opinion of who you were, to move over to my side. I needed that. I didn't know, then, how much more I would need it as things went on.

By Sunday morning, I gave up trying to speak, and spent the day sitting in silence. It was easier that way. I heard my sister talk to my parents about lawyers and the letter I'd been sent. They reminded me that I was clever, that I could manage this. I had to play by the rules, that was all, but I was good at writing letters and I had to make sure I was clear about my side of things. I wasn't to let you steamroller me. Not any more. And my mum tutted quietly, and I felt ashamed that I had brought this to them. I had tried all my life to make them proud, and look at the mess I had made of everything.

After that first weekend with them, I had to promise my parents I'd come back for Christmas. I had a couple more weeks of work to get through, and then I was to leave London and head back north. I kept my head down at the office, and got through the days as best I could. Things at the flat stayed the same, so I worried less about you moving my things. I spent the last few days before the holidays camped at my friends' place round the corner, watching them prepare for their celebrations. Two advent calendars, two stockings slowly filling with presents. It was a slow kind of torture.

For the first time in two decades I spent Christmas with my parents. A total loser, having failed so spectacularly to construct a family of my own to spend this most family of days with. Before I went, I travelled across Hackney to your sister's house to leave you your Christmas present on the doorstep. I had no intention of seeing you, but I wanted to give you the present I'd been planning for you for weeks. It was agonising to imagine you opening it without me – would you? Or would you simply throw it away? I had to show you that I was still yours, still with you on the big days, still holding on for us.

I walked up the path to the front door and put the box down, hesitating as I thought about knocking on the door. I didn't have to: not realising I was standing there, you opened it as I prevaricated, on your way out to... where? Your lawyer's? Did they do Christmas meetings?

I started to speak but you turned back inside, slamming the door shut. I had looked you in the eye for the first time in weeks. In spite of your reaction, it was enough for me. I'd seen you jolt in response to my presence. I felt you reacting to me. And for then, for me, it was enough to realise I still had that power over you. Something remained.

Once at my mum and dad's I drank, a lot. It was easy to do, arriving late on Christmas Eve, being handed a glass, then a bottle, of wine. Gin. Port. Beer. But still not enough that I could sleep, when I eventually made my way up to what used to be my bedroom. I self-medicated, swallowing down one of the sleeping pills a helpful friend had slipped me, just in case. Good ones; they've got me off to sleep after more than one big night, they'd said. And it worked, at first, but I didn't stay under. Too-vivid dreams, too-vivid wakening, into a darkness I knew would remain even after the sun rose. Willing the sun to rise anyway, before falling back under the sheets. Falling back under.

Christmas morning. The best day of the year. My nephew once told me how unfair it was that there was only one Christmas each year, and when it was over you had to wait another 364 days for the next one. It had made me laugh, this impatient child, this fervour for the ritual and the excitement and the cloying closeness of a day spent with family. Consuming, compromising. This year, surviving.

My mum crept in to me at 9 a.m. to say that my siblings, nephews and nieces were arriving soon. I had to get up. I had to. Did I have to? She brought me coffee and worried looks, and I told her I'd be OK. What else could I say?

As soon as was decent I had a drink. 11 a.m. And so I got through the morning in stages, measured out in measures: one for the present unwrapping, one for the nibbles, one for the first go at new games, one for the chatting, one for luck. I was managing. I was numb. I was desperate to feel altered.

I thought many times of what you were doing, whether you wondered or cared who I was spending this day with. I knew the routine for Christmas at your sister's, could imagine exactly what each hour would contain. I wanted so much to be there, although I'd always hated it. It made me smile, then, thinking that I was longing for the chaos and the coarseness of a day with your family. How low could I go?

I was drunk enough by the time my dad announced Christmas lunch was on the table. Which helped, I think, when I walked into the dining room and saw our wedding photo on the sideboard, among the other smiling couples, my siblings all proudly standing beside their other halves. I walked over to snatch it down, and – dramatically, I knew – marched out of the room with it, shoving it under a box in the utility room while my mother wrung her hands and apologised. I forgot it was there, I'm so sorry, I should have thought.

It doesn't matter, Mum. It doesn't matter now.

I don't remember much more. I tried to call you, knowing I'd only get your voicemail. There was another humiliating moment over dinner when one of the kids asked where you were, and when they'd see you again, and I felt my face crumple, my bottom lip wobble like a child. Pathetic. In front of all of them. And no one knew what to say or what to do, no one made a move towards me. Until finally my niece looked right at my mum and said: Nana, you need to give J a hug. And so she took the prompt and got up from her chair and came across to put her arms around me. It was more than I could bear.

I left the next day, driving back down the motorway with a hangover and a boot full of presents I hadn't opened. I felt like shit. I had the radio on loud, and I was driving fast, looking forward to getting back to the flat and barricading myself in against the world. It took me a minute or two to realise there was a policeman on a motorbike tailing me, flashing his lights. My heart jumped in my chest, and I raced through a mental list of what I had done. Was I too drunk still? What speed was I going? What the fuck else could go wrong?

I pulled over into the slow lane and was gestured off at the next exit, and told to stop the car. The officer got off his bike and came round to my window. Do you know you were speeding? he said. Actually I did, but I thought it best not to mention it. And I've run your licence plate and you don't have a valid MOT. What? I don't understand.

And then of course I knew: it was the one thing you insisted you looked after, the car, taking great pride in filling up the screenwash and checking the tyre pressure whenever we went away in it. We'd put it in your name when we bought it, since you had more years on your licence; you said it made sense. I was glad you wanted to be in charge of something. I should have fucking known you couldn't do it.

Sorry, officer, my wife deals with all the car stuff and she didn't let me know the MOT was due, because we've just split up and I...

My voice cracked, and I stopped talking, looking down at the floor and praying that this man would take pity on me. To his credit, he look horrified as I tried to get myself together, hiccuping back a sob and wiping my nose with the back of my hand. I've just spent Christmas with my parents and I can't tell you how shit everything is. I'm sorry I was driving fast. I was just trying to get home and get away from everyone...

He was a decent man, I could tell. He took a step back and said he couldn't do anything about the MOT but he wouldn't give me a speeding ticket on top. Just the one fine to pay. He scribbled out a ticket and told me to get the MOT done as soon as I could. And not to drive again until I had. And then he sort of patted me, and said good luck with it all. Take care.

It felt like the kindest thing anyone had done for me for a long time. I got back into the car and watched him drive away, then put my head on the steering wheel and sat, motionless, for a long time. I didn't know whether to start the car again. I didn't know where I wanted to go. I had nowhere I needed to be, after all.

Eventually I started the engine and pulled back onto the road. I thought about telling my friends about what had happened over a pint. That even after you'd left me I was still picking up the pieces of your ineptitude, your inability to keep on top of things. Or had you done it on purpose, knowing I was still using the car, hoping I'd get into trouble? I drove on, raging at you while wanting more than anything to laugh about it with you. To be heading home to you.

Instead, when I got back to the flat there was something else there to greet me. A fat brown envelope sat on the doormat. Hand delivered. By you? Or did you pay a bit extra so that I'd get it over the holidays? Merry fucking Christmas, wife. Here's to a happy new year.

Friday 18 March

J lost it again last night. We went out after work, and I wanted us to have a quiet dinner, no fighting, maybe even sex if I felt like it. I wanted a chilled weekend, starting with some time where we could be nice to each other.

We met at a restaurant I wanted to try, and at first things were fine, because I worked hard to keep it light and not talk about any of the subjects I knew would spark an argument. I feel like I'm treading on eggshells all the time. I'm exhausted. J said sorry for being at work so much, but I didn't believe it. J used to have all the time in the world for me, but since starting this new job, there's so much less time for us. I feel like I'm an afterthought, an irritation.

I'm sure there's something going on with someone at work. There are too many mentions of this same woman, a 'good friend', for it not to be more significant. I don't trust that J won't do something to hurt me.

Dinner was OK until I mentioned money. I was putting too much into our joint account, and never had enough for myself. I didn't think it was fair. I said I wanted J to put in an extra couple of hundred pounds to get us back in the black. I don't like being in debt, and I don't know why we have to have payments set up for things I don't use: Spotify, BT Sports, the Wi-Fi. I don't think it should be up to me to pay for all this stuff. That was all it took to kick things off.

As usual, J got angry and said we should share everything equally, and there's lots of things in the house one or other of us doesn't use but still pays for. This isn't true, but I got scared that things would get too aggro, even though we were in public. Sometimes it's not enough to have other people around to stop it happening. Like that time when we were out near our house, and J grabbed me and pushed me up against a fence to 'make sure I was listening'. I remember the grip of J's hands on the waistband of my coat, either side of my hips, and trying to blank out what was happening by smiling, just a little bit. It felt safer to normalise the situation rather than shout back, or fight back. I didn't know what would happen if I did.

By the time this argument started, we'd finished our meal and I was drinking a glass of wine. J wanted to leave, but I didn't feel safe going outside. J paid the bill so we would be able to leave more quickly, and when we got outside, looked really angry. I was scared – as usual. I said I wasn't going to go home if J was going to behave like this, which just made things worse. J screamed that I would come right now and we could talk about things there, instead of making another scene in the street. I was an embarrassment, apparently, and was acting like a mad person by refusing to go back to the flat.

I said I would rather go back to my sister's house, and began to walk away towards the tube. The street was quite empty, and I was scared J would follow me. In the past, J has become furious when I make contact with my sister, saying I treat her like my lover and share secrets with her that shouldn't be shared. I do tell my sister everything. Why shouldn't I? She says that J is jealous, and tries to control me. I think she's right, and I think it's got worse over time.

I called my sister but I got no reply, which spun me into a bit of a panic. I didn't want to go home – I couldn't – but I didn't want to walk the streets until I could get hold of her either. I wanted a good night's sleep, and I wanted peace and quiet, without the drama of J's anger. I am so tired of being made to feel like I am the problem. I used to feel like I was important, the centre of J's universe. But that's gone, I don't know exactly when. I keep trying to bring the focus back to us, and what we both want, but J is becoming more and more distant. And more selfish. It's all work, and making time for friends. It's never about me any more.

I thought about my options, and decided that I would book into a hotel for the night. I could just sleep and chill out, and not spend the night being shouted at or cajoled into backing down. I would be safe. So I rang a couple of nearby Premier Inns and the one at Smithfields had a room free that wasn't too expensive, so I said I was on my way. When I got there, the receptionist was really kind, like she knew what was happening to me. I wondered what kind of relationship she was in. When I got to my room, I turned my phone off, because I'd had eight missed calls from J and I didn't want my sleep interrupted by any more.

In the morning, I turned my phone back on, and listened to my messages. There were five from J, saying they'd expose me as a lunatic to my friends, as unhinged, someone who didn't give a shit about anyone but themselves. There were threats, as usual: to call my mum telling her I was missing, to call the police. I felt sick. Then there was a message from my mum, asking if I was OK. I couldn't believe J had actually called her, and got her so worried. What a selfish prick. It was obvious I just wanted some space by myself, and that I would come back when J had calmed down.

I called my mum and told her I was absolutely fine, and that I'd been a bit drunk at a friend's house and decided to stay there for the night. J had just got confused about what the plans were. I really hadn't wanted to drag her into any of this. I didn't want her to know I was having such a hard time, although I could tell she didn't believe what I was saying to her.

I headed home feeling cross and upset and frightened. I didn't know what J would do when I got there: the last message was incoherent and furious, and I'd deleted it as soon as it had started playing. I didn't want it on my phone. I got to our front door, and tried my key in the lock. It didn't move. I was confused, and tried for a while to make it work, before I realised that the door was double-locked from the inside. Then I heard J call down from the stairs at the top of the landing, telling me that I couldn't get in, and I should go away for the rest of the weekend. Oh my god, I thought. I couldn't get into my own home. What if J changed the locks? Or decided to move my belongings out? I felt incredibly vulnerable, and I had to fight back tears. I was completely defeated.

I spent ages banging on the door, pleading with J to let me in. At first J argued back, all the usual stuff: find yourself some other sucker to sleep with if you don't want to come home to me, that kind of thing. Then, nothing. I didn't want the neighbours to see what was happening – it was humiliating – so I didn't shout too loudly. But after a long period of silence from inside, I knew I'd have to get some help. I thought about the Nigerian family next door, and how they'd look at me if I explained J had locked me out. They'd never completely warmed to us after we'd rolled in one morning from a big night out, just as they were heading out to church. I remember feeling really embarrassed, but J said it was all part of living in a multicultural area and it was good that they were exposed to different lifestyles. It would loosen them up a bit. They were kind people but I knew they'd be at least a bit judgemental and I was desperate not to show anyone else the mess I was in. So I decided to call the police. It was really my only option.

It didn't take very long for the squad car to arrive. Two officers got out and walked up the path. I was sitting on the doorstep. They were very kind, and listened as I explained again what had happened. They said that they were going to come up into the flat with me, and make sure I was safe. If anything happened, they could arrest J, so I wasn't to worry. One of the officers took my keys off me and tried the door, which opened straight away. I started to cry.

We walked up the stairs and into the living area, where J was standing, holding a cup and trying to look innocent. I could see the outline of a faint smile, hidden beneath pretend concern. One of the police officers explained that I'd called them because I couldn't get access to the flat, but that they'd been able to open the door when they'd arrived. J said that was because the latch had been put on last night as a security measure, and then taken off again when I'd arrived home and started shouting. I probably hadn't heard that, because I was making so much of a racket.

I could feel the mood in the room shift, J sharing a smile with the two officers. I saw a kind of narrowing of their eyes, heard the faint sound of irritation creep into their voices. I could feel myself not being believed.

J apologised to them, saying it was awful that we'd wasted their time. One of the officers took me back downstairs, and asked me if I felt safe to stay. I was shaking, quite violently, but I said yes. I could see that he wanted to get away by now. It wasn't the heroic rescue scene that they'd no doubt pictured as they blue-lighted their way over.

Another madwoman, they'd laugh later on. That's what J said they'd say, anyway, after they'd left. You realise you made yourself look absolutely mental?

Sunday 29 May
I was hoping things were getting better. But we went to a friend's birthday party this weekend, and I could see they were worse than ever. Others saw it too.

J was in a really bad mood when we set off. We were driving to the coast, where our friends were having a big party: over a hundred people, a rented venue, bands, DJs and lots of J's friends. I wasn't really looking forward to it, as I knew a lot of them would end up getting really wasted and J would probably be dragged into it. I hate it when J is out of it. I've said so, many times.

J had to make a speech, which I could tell was going to be a problem. We'd had a really busy week in the run-up to the party, and J was especially stressed by work, and hadn't done any prep for the party. I was feeling anxious before we'd even set off that all of it would come back on me.

At first it was lovely to be there. It was hot and sunny, and we all met at the beach and sat outside the pub on the sands. I was really glad that two of my closer friends had turned up, and I told them I'd been worried I'd be on my own if they hadn't come. They were really sweet: they said they'd make sure I had a good time.

J said it was time to head to our Airbnb, which we were sharing with Nancy and Mel. I didn't really feel like it. I was enjoying being outside and I wanted to have another drink. As usual, I was made to feel really guilty about not jumping immediately when J said go. I overheard some nasty comment being muttered and thought I'd better get up to avoid things getting louder, and embarrassing. Nothing too awful could happen anyway, once we got back to the Airbnb place. There would be other people around for the whole afternoon.

J was silent on the way there. I asked how the day had gone so far, and was snapped at, so decided not to talk any more. I was looking forward to J getting out of the way to start on the speech, leaving me to just chill out for a bit with my book. But as soon as we got inside, the criticism started: why did I have to drink so much, why was I so loud, why couldn't I just help J out by coming when asked, didn't I know how stressful this all was? Our friends were in the garden, and I really didn't want them to hear us having yet another argument. They'd been around too many times when J had started in on me like this.

I said there was nothing to be that stressed about, it was just a speech at a birthday party – no big deal. That's when J really flipped out, telling me that it wasn't about the stupid party, it was everything else: things piling up at work, jobs around the flat I never helped with. Another tirade of accusations and self-pity, with me to blame for everything.

Nancy came in from outside just then. J stomped upstairs. Nancy could tell I was upset, and asked what was happening, so I told her we'd had another fight. I said I was really tired of the constant criticism. I was struggling to keep myself together by this point. It was really good to hear Nancy say that J was being out of order, and I deserved to be treated so much better. We headed out to the garden together and Nancy poured me a glass of wine which helped me relax a bit. I decided to put myself first and have a good time.

I didn't see J for the rest of the afternoon. I sat in the garden with Nancy for an hour or so, and then more friends came round to the house and we decided to head out to get some food. I called up the stairs to ask J to join us but got no reply. I felt relieved, to be honest, more than anything else.

The party was fancy dress, so when we got back from dinner I headed up to our room to get my costume together, and check on what was happening. J wasn't there. We were supposed to get ready together, but instead I was on my own listening to Nancy and Mel in the next room laughing as they helped each other get dressed.

I called J's phone but got no reply. So fuck it, I thought. Just go on your own, and have a good time. I put on my outfit, checked my phone, decided to leave it at the rental and headed out to the party.

When I got to the venue, J was there with a face like thunder. I felt immediately that familiar sense of dread, but went over to try to be appeasing, to calm things down. How's it gone? I asked. J was horribly sarcastic: I've been here most of the afternoon helping to set up but yeah, thanks for asking and thanks for your help with the speech. You're a real support, you know? I said I wasn't going to be spoken to like that; if J had wanted help then simply asking for it would have been enough. I'd had no messages and no way of knowing what was expected of me. I wasn't a mind-reader.

J strutted off, and I watched from across the room as our friends piled in and J suddenly lit up, the life and soul of the party. My heart sank. J hadn't wanted *me* at all. The cry for help wasn't about one partner needing support from the other: J wanted flattery and adoration, it didn't matter who it came from. It could have been anybody. I am so sick of it having to be me.

The party got going, and I stayed at the edge of the room, chatting with a few people, feeling pretty outside of things. After a while I could see J trying to catch my eye, smiling, holding a pair of dark glasses in one hand, a glass in the other. I wondered how many had already been drunk. I could see the alcohol taking hold, softening the lines of J's face, usually so tense. I think it was noticing this that made me drop my guard. I felt protective; I wanted J to relax. I was glad to receive a smile, to feel some warmth being sent my way. I wanted us to feel like we used to. I was desperate for that.

When we first got together, I used to love going out with J. I loved being part of the couple we were, and I loved seeing how happy everyone was for us. J has lots of friends who demand a lot of time and energy, and a gang of ex-girlfriends who still hang around, but in the early days I got all the attention. I never felt jealous of anyone, I never felt lonely. I knew I was the centre of J's world, I was told that over and over. We used to rent this little place in Dorset that we pretended was our second home, and we'd spend weekends there drinking red wine and having sex on the rug in front of the fire. Or once, in the garden outside, not caring who saw. It was our little bubble, a hideaway, and it felt like the best place on earth. Just the two of us. I think J's always liked me best when we're alone.

I wish things were still like that. I wish J wanted me on my own, not just as a prop in a room full of people at a party. The evening was long, and stressful. People got slowly wasted, speeches were made – including J's, which went fine. J got choked up halfway through it, and then felt embarrassed afterwards, wouldn't stop asking me if it had been OK. I said it was fine. People liked to see other people's weaknesses.

The party started to wind up around 1 a.m., and the venue had to be cleared by 2 a.m. I could tell J wasn't ready to go to bed, and I dreaded having to join the after-party crowd. I was so over late-night chats with wide-eyed, rigid-jawed friends of J's. What was the point of getting so out of it you couldn't talk properly? The same stupid in-jokes and rambling stories, bodies strewn about, the sun coming up. We'd had this conversation lots of times. Stop being so judgemental, J always said. They like to have a good time, and so do I. It's fun.

It wasn't fun, it was boring. But J didn't want to miss out – of course. I was made to feel bad for suggesting we just go to bed, that I was tired and we'd had a good night. I wasn't going to back down, and I wanted J to come with me. I didn't want to be on my own. I'd spent all day acting like a single person, a gooseberry with our coupled-up friends. I wanted J to put us first. It didn't feel too much to ask that J simply come home with me.

But no. J wanted to spend time with friends from way back, was entitled to a blowout, had been looking forward for weeks to catching up with everyone. There was no real discussion, just an ultimatum: come with me, or go home. What was the point in competing? I wouldn't win. So I walked away, and told J not to bother coming back to the rental at all. I didn't want to be woken up at a stupid time, I didn't want the empty apologies, and I didn't want to see in another day feeling shit about myself.

It feels like parenting. And it makes more of a joke of J's idea that we should start a family. I don't want to look after another child when I already have to do so much to look after J. You can't be a parent if you can't even look after yourself.

In the morning, I woke up in a half-empty bed. J hadn't come back. I cried, lying back against the pillow, feeling the tears run down past my temples and into my hair. J had chosen a late night out over me. It was pretty clear where I stood on the list of priorities. I called J's mobile, not expecting an answer, but J picked up: I'm at Helen's, I slept on the floor, you told me not to come back so I didn't...

I'd created the perfect excuse for bad behaviour, in other words.

I need to get out of this relationship. I am being made to feel smaller and smaller, like I just don't matter at all. I spent the whole weekend either worrying about J being near me, or disappearing. This isn't a good way to live, I know that. I feel really low. I don't know how much longer I can keep hiding parts of myself, pushing down my feelings, ignoring J's abuse.

I took vows when we got married, but I can't be held to them when the person I married doesn't care about them at all. I keep asking myself why J has changed, but if I'm really honest with myself, the control and the moods that are so obvious now were always there in the background. I didn't notice them for so long because J has always been so good at the demonstrative stuff: putting me on a pedestal but not really *seeing* me. I was swept up by the romance, and the sweet talk. J always said we looked good together, but looking good isn't enough. I haven't felt good for such a long time. I've just been holding everything together. I don't think I can do it for much longer. And I don't think I ought to: I deserve better.

Monday 8 July
I think I've got to the final straw. We went away last week with Nancy and Mel and my sister and Tom, and it was awful. I just don't think I can do this any more. Usually J is horrible to me in private, but all smiles in public. Last week the mask slipped. Everyone saw the meanness and the control and the belittling of me. I was so embarrassed.

78

We all spent the week in a rented house in Suffolk. From the start J wasn't happy about it, saying it was too expensive, we could have gone somewhere interesting, why did we want to spend precious holiday time in the land of middle-class social climbers with no imagination. J said I spend too much time imagining myself as something I'm not. The criticism of my background is always there, the nasty asides about the working-class chip on my shoulder. My family is rock solid; I know they'd always be there for me. It makes J feel insecure when I say these things. J's family are uptight and middle class; there are walls of silence around so many of their issues. It's not like that in my family. We talk about everything, and we say what we think. I know J finds that threatening.

We'd argued on the way up. J had started on at me about how little I contribute: I leave things that need fixing, I don't have any idea how much anything costs, J has to sort everything out… it's always the same. It doesn't seem to matter that my job takes all my energy. People need me, and I work so hard for them. I don't have the headspace for stupid little jobs around the house. I tuned it out, focusing instead on the long grey stretch of the motorway, eventually giving way to smaller roads, too many roundabouts and, finally, a view of the sea. The house looked cool, and by the time we got there my sister and Tom were already settled in, which was such a relief. I could relax a little bit; J would behave better in company.

Nancy and Mel turned up about an hour later, and the first evening and the next day were fine. I could see J was still tense, which always makes me feel anxious, but there was plenty of drinking, we made nice food and we had a good walk around the coast. I made sure that we ended up in a nice old pub. I knew that would make J happy.

Everyone was a bit pissed by the time we got back to the house that evening. They all went to bed early except me and J, and my sister, who cracked open a bottle of Tanqueray. She was really making me laugh, telling a story about running into one of her kids' friend's parents at a karaoke bar just as she really went for it with a Tina Turner number. J stood up with an eye roll at the end of the anecdote. I was furious; it was so rude. I hoped my sister hadn't noticed, but I saw her face fall. She followed J into the kitchen where the bottle of gin stood on the counter, and J was refilling an enormous glass with it. I saw that look, she said, loud enough that I could hear her from the living room. Am I boring you? I heard J just laugh at her, and then reappear, sitting back down on the sofa as if nothing had happened. My sister wasn't going to let that go – I knew she wouldn't. She came back into the room and shouted: J was so arrogant, was no good for me, was making me miserable and didn't even care, or even know? I told her to stop, but I could see she was really upset. I didn't blame her.

But I didn't want her to say things to J that I'd told her in confidence. I didn't know what J would do. I'd had a long chat with my sister two weeks before the trip, and she'd said it sounded like J was abusive. I'd never really used that word before, not even in my own head. It felt terrifying, but also like a breakthrough of sorts. It had been such a relief to have someone understand what was happening to me. I'd told her about all the little criticisms, the night I'd stayed at the hotel, the police... I'd felt so ashamed, but I wanted her to know what things were really like. She was shocked, I saw that. And she was angry, too. It was inevitable, I suppose, that she'd show that anger to J at some point.

J was horribly sarcastic at first. Haven't you had a bit too much to drink, again? And: oh, here comes Sister Number Two, the really mad one. I felt sick. I couldn't say anything. It was a car crash I couldn't look away from. My sister repeated something she'd already said to me: you're isolating her from her family, we know what you're doing. We all think it. My mum is so upset about it, she never sees her any more. You won't let her. There aren't even any photos of us up in your home.

That's when J lost it, smashing a glass against the table. We all stood for a second in silence. I was shaking, and trying hard to stop myself from crying my eyes out. What the fuck are you talking about, you loon, J shouted at my sister. I hated listening to that tone of voice, the rage.

She doesn't think I'm isolating her; you know absolutely nothing about our lives. You only pop up when you need something – I've spent a lot of time listening to how unreliable you are, and how upsetting it is that you bail on plans all the time…

I was shocked to hear J lie like that. I wanted to stop the conversation. I said to J that it was unforgivable to throw a glass in anger. I was going to go outside with my sister while she calmed down, and then I wanted an apology for her. Tom appeared from upstairs then; he'd been woken up by the noise. I don't know what he'd heard exactly. I told him everything was fine, and made him go back to bed. It was humiliating enough that my sister had witnessed J's temper; I didn't want anyone else being part of it.

J looked strange, like something terrible was about to happen. I braced myself. But that night nothing else was said: J went upstairs and by the time I got there, about an hour later, was asleep. I had another drink with my sister, and she said that whenever I decided to get out, she would be there. I had to put myself first. I had to think like a single person, and just figure out the best way to leave so that I didn't end up losing everything.

In the morning, things were uneasy. The others had heard about the argument – or had heard the argument – and tiptoed around us. My sister and Tom headed out early for a day by themselves, leaving us with our friends. I suppose it was helpful: it took some of the tension away, and by the afternoon we were managing to have an OK time. We visited the seafront, went on the old-fashioned arcade games. J was distant. I was being given the cold shoulder, the usual punishment. J sought out the company of our friends, arranging a long run with Nancy the next morning, and to go to the pub in the afternoon with Mel, a whole afternoon's absence for later in the week. I suppose I was meant to feel left out.

My sister came back in the evening and we got through that night OK. Nothing more was said. I wanted to talk to her about it, but I think she'd decided not to interfere any more. I didn't blame her, but I did feel lonely. Everyone else had someone to chat to, to be with, either in bed after we'd all said goodnight to one another, or in the morning over breakfast. I felt completely alone. J wouldn't talk to me at all.

It was a really long week. I couldn't wait to leave, but I also dreaded going home. We've been back for the weekend and it's easier, in a way, to be here. There are ways of avoiding J, patterns that we've already established that mean I can be on my own without being attacked for it. I went to my yoga class, did some cooking, J went out for another long run... in these ways we avoid each other. I just don't know how much longer I can avoid the inevitable. I don't want to live like this. I am so alone. J just doesn't care any more. About our marriage. And especially about me.

Wednesday 24 August
J found this journal and read it. I'm not sure how much of it, but when I got home from work it was sat on the kitchen table: an accusation, a hand grenade with the pin pulled out. I knew when I saw it that it was left there as a threat. That I should be frightened. I was.

I went through the kitchen into the back garden, finding J sitting with a beer on the decking. I said hello, but didn't get a reply. Then, suddenly, J stood up and walked back into the house, hissing at me to come inside. I paused, but J was standing on the doorstep, waiting for me. It felt pointless to refuse. I walked inside the back door, which J swung shut behind me. I knew it was so the neighbours wouldn't hear what came next.

Back in the kitchen, J was struggling to stay composed. We

both looked at the journal, and I smiled at J, hoping to calm things down, but it had already begun. How could you write those things about me, why would you say that? I had no reply. I was sick and tired of J denying that there was anything wrong: the criticisms, the threats, the accusations, all of this just ignored or, worse still, normalised. J had a way of convincing me that everyone argued about the same things as us, everyone had rough patches, we just had to make more effort to see one another's side of things. Well, J had just seen my side, unfiltered. I was pretty sure it wasn't going to help us become a happier, more peaceful couple. The kind of couple I had wanted us to be.

J was getting angrier. Tell me how you can write such bullshit down. You're a fantasist; none of this actually happened. You do know that, don't you?

I wasn't listening. I was making my mind up, slowly letting a decision take shape in my brain and then getting ready to say it out loud.

J, I'm leaving you.

Finally. I actually said it.

J stopped, stood absolutely still.

I mean it, I'm leaving you. I don't want to live like this any more. I'm sick and tired of fighting.

J went white. I actually saw the change in skin tone, the colour draining away. I had imagined this moment many times, but I hadn't pictured it being like this. It made me frightened: for myself and, I realised, for J too. I was the stronger one of the two of us. I knew I would be all right.

Please don't say things like that, J said. I want to talk, sensibly, about what you wrote and why you wrote it. Threatening to leave is not sensible. It's a mean and manipulative way to avoid what we're actually talking about.

J was trying to make me angry, to make me say something that would put me in the wrong. It was a game I knew very well. It was a game I wasn't going to play now.

I repeated what I'd said: I'm going to leave you. We can't go on like this. I don't want to spend any more of my life fighting.

But I love you, and you love me, said J. Isn't that worth fighting for? I don't think I could live if you left me. I don't want to.

It was horrible. I hated that we'd come to this. We'd spoken so many times about sorting things out, but J never changed. I couldn't make that change happen on my own.

J started pleading with me. I'll do whatever you want; we could get help, we could go to counselling together. I'd suggested this myself, many times, but J had always laughed at the idea, saying we didn't need to pay some stranger £100 an hour to sit in a room in Tufnell Park and be told to remember the things that first attracted us to one another. J had always said that attraction wasn't the problem, since it hadn't ever gone away. And it was true: I still wanted J, and I knew the feeling was mutual. But that wasn't enough to hold together a marriage when everything else was such a mess.

The conversation went on and on. J kept begging me to change my mind, promising to be different, to be better. It was humiliating. I kept calm, and stuck to my lines. I said I wasn't going to change my mind.

J started sobbing, lying down on the floor and curling up into a ball. I didn't know what to do. It was appalling to watch. I'd never seen someone act with such desperation.

I knelt down, and touched J's hair gently. I found myself saying that things would be all right, we'd find a way. J turned to me, eyes wide, and I could feel my resolve crumbling. I didn't want to cause this hurt, and I didn't want to lose my marriage, and the life we'd built together: our home, our friends, our things. I just wanted to feel happy again.

I had to take some time out. I decided to leave for the weekend, to go to my mum's. I told J I was going to think about things; I needed time to work out what to do. I could see the relief spread across J's face, thinking that I'd changed my mind.

I hadn't. I didn't think I had. I couldn't think straight with J in the same room. I felt crowded out of my own thoughts. I wanted to see my mum, and I wanted some quiet. Most of all I wanted to be away from J.

I said I was going to pack a bag, then get going, and that I'd be back on Sunday and we could talk again then. J was almost jubilant, saying that we'd work it all out. I said nothing was certain; I didn't want to feel railroaded. We had a lot to sort through. J agreed, and then brought up my journal, saying we still needed to talk about that. I paused, and J quickly said it could wait – or we could just drop it: just come home on Sunday and we can make a fresh start.

Sunday 28 August
When I left the flat last week, I'd texted my mum on the way to the train station. I hadn't explained anything, just said I fancied a weekend with her and was she around. 'Of course,' came the reply, 'I'm always here.' It was only then I allowed myself to cry.

It was such a relief to get to her house. Mum had waited for me to arrive so we could have dinner together. Dad was already in bed, propped up watching the portable TV at a deafening volume. The smell of home and the taste of her cooking was exactly what I needed to calm myself down. She opened a bottle of cheap red wine – I always smile when Mum brings out one of her Echo Falls or Ernest & Julios – and had some with me. We watched the telly after dinner and Mum caught me up on how different family members are getting on, who is doing well at the bowling club and who won at the bingo recently. We both nodded off a bit, waking up when the news at ten came on. I got up to go to bed. Mum wasn't long behind me: I heard her shuffling around in the bathroom. The next thing I knew it was morning.

I couldn't decide whether or not to tell her what was happening. She'd asked after J, of course, and I said we were both fine, everything was going along as usual. Mostly, that's true. That's the problem.

It was good to be at home. Dad has become very quiet in the last few years, so it's much easier to have Mum to myself. It must be much easier for her too. I know he'd do anything for us, that's what he always says. But it's so much better now that he's older, and frail. He still gets excited about Christmas, but that's about it. He's always loved Christmas, loved having us all around. And he hated it after we left home, I remember that. I think that's when he got worse towards my mum, putting her down more, all that. J's says I'm like him now, critical all the time. I've always been scared that I will turn out like my dad, so it's a really mean thing to say. I think J does it on purpose.

Dad always said that if you're unhappy, there's always something else around the corner. He never stayed where things annoyed him, or when he thought he could do better. J thought he was abusive towards Mum, but he didn't understand how much he loved her. He'd have been lost without her. She's the one who'd be all right on her own.

Me and Mum decided to spend the day at the beach, make the most of the sunshine, leaving my dad with the paper and the afternoon sport. I love the beach in summertime, and the weather was brilliant. After breakfast we headed to the shops to get some picnic stuff and the papers. We spent the day on deck chairs, reading and chatting, and just before we left my mum said something that made me stop short. We were talking about my dad, and she suddenly said she had thought about leaving him when me and my sister were children, but hadn't gone through with it. I don't know where it came from, this revelation. I don't know if she had spoken to my sister and she knew what was happening to me. And I don't know if she was telling me to do as she had done – or the opposite.

We headed home and had another quiet evening in, and by the morning I'd made up my mind. I left Mum and Dad's after breakfast, and was home by midday. I let myself into the flat, and found J on the sofa, reading the paper. It was such a familiar scene. I've spent so many mornings sitting like that, reading with J, drinking coffee together. It's always been one of my favourite things.

You're back, said J. Yes. I'm going to give it one more try. But there are conditions this time. Non-negotiable. We have therapy together. You could also have sessions on your own. You stop working so much. You make time for me, and for us. And you stop criticising me and putting me down. I won't take it any more. You have to start treating me like you love me.

J leapt up to hug me.

I cringed. I hope it wasn't obvious.

I have made the decision to stay. I want to see if we can salvage something from our years of being together. I listened to what my mum said. I've thought about what I stand to lose by leaving. And most of all I've thought how difficult it would be to extricate myself. How persuasive J would be. Has been.

I've made my bed. I will lie in it, for now. But I'm ready to change my mind, and J knows it. I've left no room for bullying and bad behaviour. That is my plan.

January

You'd been busy, I'll give you that. How sweet that you'd spent the run-up to Christmas preparing such a gift for me. And how carefully thought out it was, too.

'Our client has taken advice in respect of a financial settlement and wishes to put forward a proposal. Placing the house on the market does put an element of time pressure on the need to reach a concluded settlement and, unfortunately, our client does not believe that mediation would be possible.'

Of course not. Talking would be far too human a way to proceed. Better do this via a proxy, you fucking loon.

'Her wish is to ensure a swift conclusion to proceedings in the interests of preserving your mutual assets and reducing the emotional impact of protracted proceedings.'

Ha! Good start, then. No better way to mitigate against emotional impact than getting a lawyer to write a letter. Even more so if that letter sets out a distribution of everything you own in a clinical and impassive way. And definitely if it attempts to fucking screw you out of your money, your belongings and your future.

'As you are aware our client has made a much larger contribution to the purchase of the property and will clearly need to secure most of the equity in the home both to reflect this and to ensure that she can purchase a suitable home. We therefore propose a split of the net equity after sale with three-quarters going to our client, and the remaining amount to you. This would mean you are left with considerably more than you came to the marriage with.'

Wow. My marriage has turned me a tidy profit – that's nice! Except we've been together for six years, and the house will sell for at least double what we paid for it, and while you put down more money at the start, I fucking built the house. Actually built it, giving up work and sinking everything I had into making it the home we wanted. You wanted. How efficiently you've excised all that from these sham negotiations.

I hadn't ever felt the rage I experienced as I read to the end of the letter. At its white-hot centre was the outrage, the sheer injustice, of your misrepresentations. A narrative I'd never heard before: how you owned everything, were owed everything. I wondered when you'd started telling this story. Was it just to your lawyer, or was it to other people? Had you actually started believing it, in order to justify behaving like such a stone-cold bitch?

I raced upstairs, dragging the ladder out from behind the washing machine, yanking it in place under the loft hatch. I scrambled up it and opened the door in the ceiling, hauling myself up and scrabbling around in the dim light until I found our wedding box. I took it back down the ladder and downstairs, putting it on the kitchen table while I thought about what to do next. I wanted to set it all on fire right there on the table. To have you come home to its charred remains, and a black hole in the wooden surface on which it sat. I imagined how upset you'd be. It was so tempting.

But I couldn't go through with it. What a pussy. What was stopping me? Someone else coming in and seeing it, I suppose. I was beginning to see that I had to cover my actions so that you couldn't twist them. I didn't know, just then, that I was much too late for that.

I took the photo album out of the box, rummaged in a drawer for some matches, and then grabbed a bottle – rum, I think – off the bar. Crouching in front of the fireplace, I lay the book down in the grate and splashed the alcohol over it. It hurt. It caused me a physical pain to know I was about to annihilate the only material record of our wedding day we had. I wanted it to hurt you too, so I struck the match and dropped it. Flames. It took less than a minute to turn to ash. And as it did, I fell into a pile beside the fireplace. I was burned out too. Spent. I'd hoped for some kick of twisted pleasure from seeing our entwined images burn, but it wasn't enough. So I stood up and stalked round the house, looking for things from our wedding day. I wanted to destroy all of them.

There was a big canvas in the spare room, made for us by our friends for our wedding, the two of us photoshopped into a beach scene, draped over one another, holding umbrella-topped coconut drinks. Do you remember how much we loved that, when we saw it propped up at the reception? Do you remember any of that day, now?

I ripped it off the wall. I took it downstairs and stood it up against a chair. Then I took the carving knife from its block and slashed it, a huge rip across the middle. I won't lie: it felt good. Seeing the blade slice open that image of us was some kind of small release. So I did it again. And again, stabbing at your picture as the fabric fell apart, imprecise but intended parries at your face, your smile... especially that fucking smile.

I only stopped because the knife broke. The blade snapped from the handle and I froze, puzzled, staring at the space where the silver shard had been. I was angry. I didn't want to stop. I swore at the tattered remains of the canvas and stamped downstairs to dump it by the bins, relishing the thought of you coming home and seeing what I'd done to it.

I wasn't finished. I went into our bedroom where, either side of the bed, I'd hung a picture of us in our wedding gear, and a framed CD of the songs I'd put together for you when we first met. I smashed my fist into the photo first, pulling back when the glass didn't break to ram my knuckles at it again, and again, until it gave way. And then I punched it one more time to make sure it shattered all over the floor. I watched as blood began to drip from my knuckles, and then headed around the bed to do it again. The glass case of the CD frame shattered immediately. The disc fell to the floor, and I stamped on it. Blood trickled from my hand. It felt good. I went out to the landing, and surveyed the photographs arranged on the walls there. Slowly, methodically, I drove my fist into every one of them, not feeling the pain in my hand, knowing I was being very, very mad. It pleased me.

I only stopped when I ran out of things to break. By then, the pain had started to rise in my hand and travel up my arm. I shuffled through the broken glass and wood on the floor, going back downstairs, noting dispassionately the red drops that followed me. I sat at the kitchen table and let a small pool of blood collect on the floor, beneath my hand, hanging limply now at my side. I felt satisfied. I had made visible, to some small degree, the pain that I lived with. It was dripping onto the floor. It was real.

I thought about you coming in here, seeing the blood, worrying what had caused it. You'd know it was mine. You'd be frightened. It did look frightening, I'd made pretty sure of that.

I wanted to see your face when you saw it all. I wanted that badly.

I realised my heart hurt. Actually physically hurt, a pain in my chest in the place where it continued, in spite of my lack of wanting, its regular beat. I wondered, disinterestedly, if I'd have a heart attack. I thought about those elderly people who just stop living when their spouse passes away after forty, fifty, sixty years together. How people say they died of a broken heart. Did this pain in my chest explain why the heart is such an emblem of love? Not because it flutters and swoons in the first throes of passion, but because it contracts and constricts when your lover leaves. It's not so romantic, this explanation of an unreliable organ. The broken heart, a stress-related arrhythmia.

I got up and got out of the house, getting into the car and deciding, after I'd set off, to drive to Zed's. I needed to show someone what I'd done. There's no point demonstrating your pain if there's no one there to witness it. It was hard to grip the wheel with my right hand, so I let it hang by my side and used my left one to steer and change gear, and eventually to pull up the handbrake when I got to Zed's street. Then again, to push the buzzer. To open the door and press for the lift. I wondered if I'd done myself permanent damage, remembering how much you'd loved my hands. The memory made me jump. I hadn't thought of you being anything but a bitch for such a long time now.

Zed answered the door and said 'fuck'.

Nice to see you too.

What the fuck have you done?

Can I come in?

Yes, get in, you idiot. Kit is here, I'm making her dinner.

Oh god, I'm sorry, I'll go.

I looked over Zed's shoulder and could see through to the living room: the Christmas lights, the table laid with small bowls of nuts and olives and glasses of wine. Inexplicably, it was still Boxing Day.

Sorry, I shouldn't have come. I didn't know what to do.

Get in here. Sit down. Tell me what happened.

Zed pulled shards of glass out of my hand, carefully, listening as I explained what I'd done and why. The settlement offer. The way it had been written, like I'd hit a jackpot. The absolute bullshit of it.

I sank everything I had into that flat, I said to Zed. I gave up my job to make sure we had the house she wanted. It was all my own work. *And* I still earned money. I freelanced. I didn't sleep more than five hours a night for weeks when we first moved in. There was so much to do, and I knew it was my responsibility to get it done. She was hardly going to pitch in and help, was she?

I lost both my grandparents in the year I built that house. I put all their inheritance money into buying things we hadn't been able to afford. She's a fucking liar. She's mad. I won't let her screw me over. I can't believe she's got a lawyer. How fucking mental is that? She won't talk to me, but she'll give her fucking story to a lawyer and let them try to annihilate me instead.

She's blocked my number, do you know that? I'm fucking married to her, and she's blocked my number.

Jesus, she's moving fast, I'll give her that, said Zed. Kit hovered in the background, pensive, muttering sympathetic words. They felt sorry for me. It was gratifying. I was a victim; they could see how much distress I was in. The blood and the glass and the pain. I felt vindicated.

I let Zed finish patching up my hand and then decided to leave them to it. I wanted to have a drink, and was happier with the thought of doing that alone. I drove home, and walked inside to survey the damage I'd done. A new plan started to form inside my head, and I felt the self-pity begin to drain away. If you were going to try to take everything, I was going to make sure I was one step ahead, all the way, baby. I was going to move things out. And I was going to start right now.

It felt so good to have a plan. Every time I faltered, and allowed myself to think about our flat stripped of our belongings, becoming the empty shell that I feared above all else, I returned to the letter from your lawyer, rereading it, letting it fuel my activity. I swept up the remains of our framed memories, wiped away the blood, and was pleased with the empty walls, the clarity that formed when the stuff was moved away. I went to bed and started making lists in my head of what needed to be done: packing boxes, removal men, storage. It was the best night's sleep I'd had in a long time.

In the morning, I started making calls. I asked for quotes from several removal companies for the first available date: 2 January. Most of the men I spoke to sounded sad not to be able to help me sooner. I wondered if they were trapped at home with in-laws, straining to get out, casually suggesting to their wives that a bit of extra money, earned in this strange week between Christmas and New Year, might be a help. Being refused.

I booked a storage unit. They asked me how much space I'd need. I couldn't answer. How much space does a life fill up? We settled on the smallest unit and said we'd reassess when I arrived. Nice people. Everyone was so helpful. I remember thinking that they must see all kinds of things come through their doors: relationships beginning and ending, dead people's belongings being tucked away to gather dust, babies' cribs and buggies being saved for the next time. I wanted to tell them what was happening to me, that I wasn't moving anywhere nice from their place. That I wasn't planning anything at all, actually. This was as far as I'd got. But they didn't ask questions. I guess you wouldn't, working there. It wouldn't be often that you'd enjoy the answers.

I was due back at work, having taken only the bank holidays off. It was both good and bad. I had a place to be for the rest of the endless holiday week, could work long days and be absorbed without having to think about you, or talk about us. I rang your phone often, hearing it go straight through to your voicemail, letting me know I was still blocked. In spite of how angry it made me, I couldn't stop myself. It had been only seven weeks since you'd left, but everything was so different. I still couldn't believe that you just outright refused to talk to me, and yet… it was textbook you. You had made your statement, and you had declined any discussion. You were so sure that you were right. Aren't you always?

I wrote you long emails instead. Setting out the events that I thought had been your trigger for leaving – having to guess, since there was only a vacuum, an empty space where you used to be. The only indicators I had were the terrible things I'd read in your journal: the very definition of gaslighting. I was pleased when I managed to write into coherent paragraphs my own side of things, explaining how frustrated you made me, how enraging your singular views were. I took some solace in being the better writer, at least, more able to present an argument with some flourish. I knew you wouldn't be able to match me, head to head, via this form of exchange. I should have guessed you wouldn't even try.

*

I got to the end of Friday's office hours and headed home. I'd made a rough assessment of how much time I had, and how much more I would need to get everything packed and ready. I was itching to get started. Having a plan had given me a purpose, and I was running on a new, frenetic energy. I drove the car round to the local Big Yellow storage unit to buy a stack of boxes, tape and bags. I felt like I was planning for a murder, putting my kit together meticulously. It wasn't an altogether unpleasant thought.

I had to get everything done before the movers arrived on 2 January, three days from now. And I knew you'd be back at the flat the following day, as per your edict. You'd return to a stripped-out house, and might finally see that what you were doing was insane. It would be awful, for you, to walk in and find that. It was something I'd pictured myself, many times, in the frenzied dreams I'd have where I'd wake up shouting your name. I was terrified and delighted by the idea of your reaction. It spurred me on.

I set about the packing with a grim determination, starting upstairs with the bathroom, which seemed the least daunting. I wouldn't take anything that was solely yours and I would be fair about the rest. I was already scared that your lawyers would find some way to screw me for moving stuff out, and I didn't want to look like an arsehole either. I knew you'd tell people I'd done this, and I wanted to be one step ahead of you: I would show that I'd only taken what was rightfully mine.

There wasn't much in the bathroom that I even wanted. I took a couple of towels, and a green medicine bottle that a friend had bought for us which I knew you liked. And the two glass vials we'd been useless at haggling for in a souk in Marrakesh, the first time we went away together. I remembered that trip: putting on a fez in bed for you one night, the smell of buttery onions mixed with incense in our riad, playing Scrabble on the roof over long breakfasts. Was it even possible that that was you? Where had you gone? Why had you gone? Why were you making me do this?

It was agonising. I moved across the landing to the bedroom, gathering things up from the cupboard at the top of the stairs. Every little thing delivered its own jab of pain, as I collected books and magazines and clothes from shelves and stuffed them into boxes. I left all your clothes, conspicuous, on the shelves next to our bed or hung in the wardrobe. Mine I removed completely, along with some bedding and small bits of furniture: the bedside table – one of my first homeware purchases from back in my earliest London days – and my old tallboy – a fixture in all the places I'd called home for even longer. I wasn't going to risk leaving anything behind that you could try to claim as your own.

I was surprised, by the time I'd finished in our bedroom, how little I had taken away. The room looked almost the same, just some new spaces on the shelves and walls but otherwise as it was before. I was disappointed. I wanted more impact.

Next door was the spare room, which I had set up as my study. My sanctuary. I'd spent more than a grand having shelves fitted by a joiner who'd made a meal about the uneven walls, but left behind a beautiful bookcase. Such a pleasing set of straight wooden lines. You'd said it was a waste of money, and had argued with me about how much it cost. I knew I'd never have been able to do such a good job, and so paid for the work myself, unable to get you to chip in. I didn't care, not really; it was one of the best things I'd ever spent money on. It had taken almost two days to alphabetise all the books we had, sifting out duplicates and finally excavating your old university texts from the mouse-shit-covered boxes in the loft. I loved being in that room of books. I'd always dreamed of it. Another dream, only recently realised, now gone.

It took a long time to pack up all the books. I took every single one, knowing that some were yours, and knowing this would upset you. I was glad. I wanted to punish you for yet another lie, the gesture you'd made by putting them all together in this room. We were in a committed relationship, and were merging. How romantic. Hadn't you meant that to show that we would stay together? Our books, and us.

At least I could make it true for the books.

I packed them all methodically away, then sat down at my desk. I was sweating from shifting now-full boxes out to the top of the stairs. Three of them sat stacked up, along with two suitcases and a heap of heavy-duty black bags. I was really doing this. The thought that I could just stop, and put it all away, back where it belonged, crossed my mind. But I thought of you again, coming in and seeing the emptiness, and I wanted that much more than I wanted to keep my things around me. I'd been careful not to mention this plan to anyone – I knew they'd try to stop me – so I was sure that you were going to get the shock I'd planned for you.

It had been difficult not to tell people what I was doing. My head was full of it, for a start, and there were friends who wanted to drop round, to see how I was doing. I'd had to refuse them. I'd also avoided phone calls from Nancy and Zed about New Year's Eve. They both had plans to be out of the country, away with their other halves' families, so were pestering me about who I'd spend the night with. Fuck them. Not thinking about me, or wondering how I'd get through a New Year's Eve alone. I was angry with them, for leaving me here. I'd be on my own. Of course I would. I'd better fucking get used to it.

Self-pity is a comfortable friend. I'd forgotten the other people that had offered to come over. I focused on all the things that confirmed my isolation.

By the time I finished I was exhausted, damp with sweat, and covered in dust. I took a beer to bed and waited for sleep to take me, racing through mental checklists of what to tackle next, once morning arrived. It seemed a long time before it did.

I woke up early. It was New Year's Eve. I was alone, in a half-naked house. It is hard to describe, now, how abject, how desperate I felt. I couldn't lift my head from the pillow. I couldn't bear to look around, at the piles of furniture and belongings now gathered at the top of the stairs, outside the bedroom door.

I got out of bed and crawled downstairs, where more boxes and bags filled the floor that used to be our living space. I could see the stupid fucking letter from your lawyer still sitting on the kitchen table, waiting for my reply. I sat on a kitchen chair, and lay my head on the solid wooden surface of the table.

I wanted it all to end.

I shut my eyes and tried to make a list of reasons to continue. I forced myself to think of my friends, my parents, the children I knew and loved; how frightening it would be for them to hear that I'd gone. My mum crying. Nancy and Zed standing over my grave, blaming themselves for not doing more.

So they fucking should.

I was here on my own and I couldn't think of a single reason to carry on.

I looked through the messages I'd sent you over the days – no, it was now weeks – since you'd left me. Not a word in reply. How could you just disappear? I wanted to do the same. I felt like there was no place for me in the world without you. It sounds pathetic – it was pathetic – but the feeling was bigger than I was, just then.

I called your phone. I knew it would go straight to voicemail but it was wrenching anyway when it did. I called your sister, leaving her a begging message, asking her to intervene so you would speak to me. Some hope, I knew.

Finally, I called her husband Tom, whom I'd always thought of as a decent enough bloke. You said you were pretty sure he was cheating on your sister, and you didn't trust him when he said he had to work every hour god sends, pretending that he needed to earn money for their renovations, their new car, their designer dog. You raised an eyebrow that only I saw when he said he had to sleep at his desk because jobs overran and his boss demanded he finish them. I didn't blame him for any of it. I just figured that he'd found a way of dealing with his life with your sister: a lively colleague who helped him forget how downtrodden he'd become. I was glad he had that bit of relief.

Tom answered his phone. Shocked to hear a human voice, I stumbled over my hello, and garbled out an explanation of trying to get hold of you, and you blocking me, and being desperate, and sorry to interrupt...

Tom stopped me. I know, J, I know all of it. Listen, I'll ask her to call you. But I wouldn't hold out much hope. And if I were you, I'd start thinking about walking away. The only way you come out of this with anything is if you do what she says. Trust me, I've heard them talking. Sorry, J. I've got to go, take care of yourself.

And then the line went dead.

I gave up. I was utterly beaten. The shred of hope I'd held onto, that somehow you'd know what I was doing, and you'd relent, and you'd come to me and soothe me and we'd work it all out... it was never going to happen. I knew it then, in that moment. And I simply didn't want to carry on.

You won't understand this. You won't believe that I was laid so low. But I was. I felt like... nothing. I had lost you, and I knew I would lose my home. I had lost any prospect of having the family I'd always wanted. I was scared that friendships were drifting from me. I felt exposed and vulnerable at work, and felt that my job, too, could be taken from me any minute. I didn't know who I was. All the things that had anchored me, and on which I'd built my sense of self... they were gone. I knew other people didn't see it: it was just a break-up, these things happen. Not the end of the world.

But it was. It ended my world. And so, in return, I wanted it all to end. I wanted, more than anything, to just stop.

To cease to be.

I went through my options for ending my life, one by one. Pills, ropes, blades, the wheels of buses or trains. I knew, in my heart, I couldn't go through with any of them. All of them involved an action, a doing, that I was simply not capable of.

I wasn't sure if there was some part of me that wanted to remain alive, or if I was just too scared of what would happen if I tried to die.

I suppose that I admitted defeat.

Slowly, I lifted my head off the table and sat upright. In time, I pulled myself up and stood over the cooker. And later still I started moving: slowly, panting, putting one thing after another in a sheath of newspaper and then into a box. And then sealing, labelling, stacking. I kept going.

I was going slowly... but I was going.

Around noon, I realised I hadn't eaten since Thursday night. I had had only beer for fuel, and now it was Saturday lunchtime and my body was protesting. Part of me was pleased. I was too broken to eat, which evidenced my torment: food was a mere frippery. I was miserable and, clearly, melodramatic.

I hadn't thought to look in the fridge, and when I did I realised that – in spite of myself – I was hungry. The fridge, though, was of no help, containing only some mangy tomatoes, old cheese... and a small bottle of cherryade. I felt overwhelmed by the idea of cooking anyway, so decided to order takeout. I didn't need to eat much; one meal today should see me through the whole process. But I should get something substantial so I didn't have to worry about it again. And alcohol. I needed to drink.

I tossed the cherryade bottle in the bin, and opened the Just Eat app on my phone. A pizza would be plenty to last me through the weekend.

Except I couldn't do it. I just could not decide which place to go with, which combination of toppings I wanted, which price deal was the best. I paralysed myself trying to figure out how to order something that I would like without paying for delivery charges. As if it mattered. I simply could not make a decision. And the longer it went on the more I felt like a hopeless loser. Who can't make a decision about a fucking pizza? An eight-year-old would have sorted it in a heartbeat. It took me almost an hour.

I finally placed my order then walked out to the shop on the corner where I bought six beers and two bottles of wine. It felt like an achievement, to have restocked with food and drink. I considered how pathetic I'd become. I wondered what you'd think if you saw me in that moment, shuffling down the road with a plastic bag of clinking bottles. I could guess. You'd said enough times that you didn't like it when I drank, that I needed to be better at looking after myself. I'd always taken it as a signal of your care, being concerned for how I was. I saw it now as just another of your systems for controlling me.

I carried on packing, getting on with the kitchen stuff, taking out cutlery and bowls and gadgets we never used but I wasn't willing to leave behind for you. It was time-consuming. There was a lot of wrapping and reorganising and fitting in of odd shapes to make the most of the box space. But I got back on track, and started to work with purpose again. There was still so much to get through.

I worked my way to the far side of the kitchen where your Kitchen-Aid stood in pride of place on the counter. The first real thing I'd ever bought you. I'd been so skint I'd paid for it on a credit card I had no hope of paying off. I didn't, for years. But you wanted one, you'd told me, so I got it for you and watched like a big kid as you'd unwrapped it and grinned and knocked me back off my haunches with your kisses.

I pulled it towards the edge of the work surface. It had seen better days, and was a bit temperamental now, sometimes coming on when you pressed the power button, sometimes not. It was broken anyway, I thought as I pulled it off the surface and watched as it hit the floor. It was really heavy. It made a pretty impressive sound on impact.

I stood over it like a murderer, wanting to make sure it was broken. Being careful to finish the job. A couple of small pieces had fallen away, but the bulk of it remained intact. So I lifted it over my head – I was amazed, even in the moment, that I had the strength to do it – and smashed it back onto the kitchen floor. The front section came completely apart, and there were gratifyingly large bits of plastic and metal now, littering the floor. Good, I thought. I was glad. I had taken something from you. It was tiny recompense for all you had taken from me.

And then something in me snapped. There was our sideboard at the far side of the room, adorned with framed pictures and a row of your coloured glass vases. More of these stood on the windowsills, where you'd put them to make the most of the sun shining through the lilacs and reds and greens of their glass bodies. You'd collected them over the years, adding to the range of colours and shapes and putting them out, pride of place, around the room. One by one, I picked them up and threw them across the full width of the flat, watching as they hit the grey stone of the fireplace, or the black tiles of the hearth, and shattered into pieces. It took a few minutes to break them all. The noise was immense, it took me by surprise. But it was so satisfying. It was freeing, fleetingly, to behave as badly as I could. To do something unhinged, mad, dangerous – all the things you said I was.

It also meant there was less to pack.

I hadn't lost my sense of humour after all.

The pizza arrived shortly after, and I ate a couple of pieces before refocusing on the packing. It was late afternoon by now. I had heard my phone ping a number of times, and knew people would be trying to get me out, to meet them somewhere for New Year's celebrations. I had no intention of responding. I was glad I had something to do, for now, that took my mind off the date, the hour. The thought of seeing in a new year that you wouldn't be a part of crushed me. I would carry on my work here, and go to bed before midnight. It was, just about, manageable.

Around 7 p.m. the buzzer went. I looked around the flat, which was in chaos. There were boxes and bags everywhere, furniture pulled out of place, and over by the fireplace a multi-coloured puddle of broken glass. I swore quietly, and considered not answering. It buzzed again, and I moved to the tiny video monitor at the top of the stairs to see who was there. If it had been one of my friends, I would have stayed still and silent until they left. But it was our neighbour, one of the beautiful couple who lived next door, smiling into the camera. They weren't part of our circle. This distance made it feel better, safer. So I buzzed her in and waited at the top of the stairs as she made her way up.

Oh my god, she said. Are you… packing? Are you OK? She had a four-pack of beers in her hand, and offered me one. Can I stay and have a drink with you? I nodded and cleared some room for us at the kitchen table, dropping my eyes as hers took in the chaos and the damage. I saw her scan across the smashed glass, the stacks of boxes, the torn paper and tape and plastic. Gallantly, she looked away.

I heard that you were separating; I saw her the other day and she told me. But this is all so fast. What happened?

I said I didn't know, not really. I told her you weren't speaking to me, she'd probably heard more about it from you than I had. I showed her the letter from your lawyers and watched the shock on her face. It was a comfort to see someone else so confused by it all. She spoke to me gently, asking what I'd been doing these past few weeks. Not prying, just concerned. I liked her a lot, and her partner. I'd been first to befriend them, and although you'd been typically aloof at first, we'd had fun with them over the years we'd spent as neighbours. Late nights of drinking, home-cooked dinners, doing errands for one another. I was glad she'd come round. I'd been feeling terribly lonely. This was better.

After a while she mentioned that they were having a party next door – just a small thing, family and a few friends from out of town. A quiet affair, she promised. Would I come? She didn't want to leave me here in this mess, not on New Year's. I found out later that Nancy had put her up to the whole thing, had been scared of my being alone this night, and had known I wouldn't answer the door to one of our group. A good friend after all. The best.

The beers inside me made it easier to say yes. I was tired, anyway. And I'd got through enough of the packing that I knew I'd get it all done before the van arrived the day after tomorrow. I had the whole of New Year's Day to sit in this chaos. So I followed her out of the flat and across to their place, and braced myself as she opened the door.

I wondered, then, what you were doing. You'd be at your sister's, of course. I considered that for a moment and felt a flash of anger, remembering the painful, endless weekends at her stripped-brick-interior, over-styled Clapton townhouse. You told me early on that she'd once been a stylist to some nineties fashion photographer, although you needn't have bothered. She never stopped referencing her heady Soho years. The tedious stories of snorting lines and running wild, delivered while she chopped out fresh white tracks to keep the conversation going. To keep her conversation going. The rest of us never got a look-in.

She was a liar, like you. She would make plans and bail on them at the last minute, leaving me to pick up the pieces as you cried and wondered why she treated you that way, as if you meant nothing. I'd defended her then, saying she was busy, it was easy to forget arrangements that had been made. I don't know why I bothered; she was always such a dick if it was us doing the un-arranging. She never stopped going on about me missing a night out with your family because of work. Easy to say when you don't ever have to work.

Whatever happened tonight, I wouldn't have to put up with the sound of her voice drilling into my head. I took a grim pleasure in that much, at least.

I walked upstairs into a room of drunk Irish people, kids running around, lights dim and music loud. The family had come over for the holidays. I smiled, rigidly. A dozen shiny faces grinned back at me, widely, as I was introduced. Drinks were brought for me. Several, at once. I wasn't sure I could handle being there after all. It was completely overwhelming, a madness of movement and energy. But it was better than being alone. And let's face it, I would have plenty of time for that.

I'm pretty sure they'd all been told what was up with me before

I'd been brought round, because a gang of women with sympathetic smiles swarmed round me, asking how I was, pressing more alcohol on me. They were lovely. They were also pretty wasted.

One of them asked me if I'd thought about where I was going to live when I moved out. It was all I could do not to walk out and take refuge back in the flat. I'd spent the past forty-eight hours packing up our home, and yet the idea of not being in it devastated me.

There's a great community in Tottenham, she said, and you get a lot more for your money. I stared at her, blinking rapidly, as if she'd suggested I move to Norwich, or somewhere even worse. Have another drink, she said. You don't have to decide now.

The party went on, kids being packed off upstairs by swaying parents, the music getting louder, midnight approaching. Suddenly it was time, and everyone started shouting down from ten. I panicked. Wanting to be invisible, I had no idea where to put myself at the moment everyone grabbed their loved one and went in for a kiss. I shifted back against a wall, and stared round the room at so many happy people, so many hugs. Someone saw me and moved over, pulling me back into the circle. I was enfolded in an Irish embrace of several different arms. The worst was over.

I relaxed a bit then, in the company of these warm and generous people. Will you have another? Try one of these? Go on, it will cheer you up. I did as I was told and the small hours went by in a blur. The same woman as before staggered over at one point and, remembering my plight, asked if I'd considered a move to Tottenham? I grinned over the top of her head, and wished you'd been there to share the joke with me. I wondered again whether you'd still be up, if you were having fun, whether you'd thought of me at all as this new year had rolled around. I was altered enough not to fully feel the stab of pain that accompanied these thoughts. I was glad of that. It was good to be numb.

I stayed until five or six, the group gradually growing smaller as some slipped away, and others headed upstairs to join their sleeping children. Some of the parents remained downstairs, glancing at their watches as they calculated how much time they had until their off-spring got up. How much time before their partner came down and berated them, bundling them into bed and out of sight.

I gathered myself for walking out into the dark morning. Our neighbours hugged me and told me to call back round later on, join them again for food and hair-of-the-dog drinks. I said yes, knowing I would not. I already felt a creeping sense of dread. I needed to sleep, and then to get on with my plan.

I got home and took a sleeping pill, then another half for good measure. I wanted oblivion, and I wanted it quickly. Lying down in our bed, in our half-empty room, I felt the now-familiar rising panic that accompanied every thought of the future. I waited, willing the tablets to do their work faster. I breathed as calmly as I could. Mercifully, it wasn't long before it all stopped.

I woke up as it was going dark. The first day of a new year. I was glad I'd missed most of it. I was alone in our home, or the shell that remained of it. I felt like a fucking loser.

I sat up in bed and felt my head throb. I thought about what I still had to do, and calmed myself down by taking a mental inventory of the rooms I'd already packed. There wasn't much left. There was a pile of shattered glass to clear away, and some bits and pieces in the living room. I wasn't going to take the bed or the sofa. I would still be staying here, on the days that you weren't, and even in my madness I knew I'd be making it difficult for myself as well as you if I took all the furniture away. Besides, I wasn't being unreasonable. I'd left the rudiments of a functioning home in place: enough pans and plates and knives and forks for lonely meals for one. The towel set we'd bought with Christmas money from your mum. The TV, and the blanket that we used to wrap ourselves up in to watch it. I'd only packed what was mine, or my share, apart from some of your books. And that was your fault anyway.

I remembered the kitchen table. It was your pride and joy. You had told me you bought it with money left to you by your nan, a way of honouring her, something you'd use and enjoy every day. You had also told me your ex, the only one that had stuck around long enough to qualify as a relationship, had mocked you for it, its size, your aspirations of hosting dinners and parties with the table at their centre. He'd said you were a snob.

What a fuckwit, I'd said of him.

He was probably right though: you did, desperately, want to be that middle-class socialite you professed to despise. While you spoke behind your sister's back about her pretentious artwork, and the sums she spent on bespoke curtains, you envied every part of it. The table was an emblem of who you thought you could be, who you wanted to present to the world. I knew how much it meant to you.

I went downstairs and pulled apart the two oak leaves that formed the tabletop, revealing the extra panel stored underneath. I took it out, and pushed the table back together. I put the wooden leaf beside the pile of boxes by the stairs, ready to go. I thought that, once you'd seen it was missing, you'd be forced to get in touch with me at last. That even if you wouldn't contact me for my sake, you would if it meant you'd get back your beloved table. I was pleased with myself for thinking of it.

I finished off packing up the living room. Records, a couple of pictures, some cushions. I swept up the pile of glass I'd created the night before, and then carried on with my cleaning. Dusting shelves, mopping floors, hoovering and polishing. It was satisfying, and deliberate. It made the house seem emptier and it emphasised that it was me, as usual, who kept the place spotless: a double whammy.

I took what remained of last night's pizza back upstairs, planning to eat it in bed and watch something mindless on my laptop. As I walked back into our bedroom I realised I hadn't checked under the bed, where we had a couple of storage boxes mostly taken up with your shoes. But there might be something there I'd forgotten, so I pulled them out to take a look. And in the first one I found a folder, shoved underneath a folded sheet. For someone so spectacularly accomplished at lying, you'd done a shit job of hiding it. Perhaps you'd wanted me to find it? I opened the folder and inside lay a pile of papers, the top sheet labelled 'transcript of a first meeting with Michelle Hendry'. Fuck. I was going to find out what your legal team had planned for me. I took the papers out, stupidly feeling almost gleeful. I thought I would get the upper hand back. I started to read, and bit by bit the room fell into darkness, only the white pages in front of me remaining, blindingly, visible.

I simply could not believe, at first, what I read on those pages. It was like having all the air sucked out of my being. I kept staring at the line 'because there is a history of emotional, psychological and physical abuse' and wondering how you dared say it. How fucking dare you?

I really wanted to hurt you then, I think. To simply snuff you out. I had been holding on by a thread for weeks, trying to make sense of why you were behaving as you were. Feeling worried for you, that you felt you had to do it this way. Actually feeling sad for you, sorry that you were so fucked up that this was the only way you felt you could proceed.

But no, I should have known. You were going to play the victim. The role in which you always excelled, a regular fucking masterclass this time. And you were going to spin it for every penny you could get.

I looked at the pages again, trying to calm my breathing. I was panicking, I could hardly catch my breath. I wanted to read the document again, but a feeling of absolute terror was taking hold of me.

I had no control over what you were saying to people. If you'd said all this to your lawyer, what were you saying to people I knew? What would they think? What would happen? Everything was spinning out of control and I had no way to get a grip on you, to stop what you were doing.

I phoned Nancy, and tried to explain what I'd found. I was talking too fast, gasping for air between sentences that tumbled out in no order. She got the drift. Should you be reading that? she asked. What the fuck does that matter? The point isn't whether I've read it or not, the point is she's fucking said it. Out loud. To a fucking lawyer!

I went through it all again, slower, trying to temper my rage, to sound reasonable in my explanations. She says we've been together for four years, not six. That's a lie I can disprove in an instant. She's an idiot, why would you say something so obviously a lie? And this thing about your birthday weekend – what a piece-of-shit story that is. She was waiting to tell me she was leaving me until *after* your weekend away, because she didn't want to ruin a fucking party? Who does that? Does she think that makes her look like a better person? She put me through the most miserable weekend of my life, running around her like a fucking lapdog because I knew something was up and she kept telling me I was imagining it. And all because she's such a fucking martyr, she cares about other people *so* much, that she didn't want to take the edge off a fucking three-day bender in a castle?

She's going to take everything, Nancy. I can see what she's doing. She's made up a story and she's going to use it to screw me out of everything.

I was ranting, I knew that. And I could see your face, I could picture you arranging yourself to look cowed, frightened. Everything I was saying was only proving you right.

Can you believe she said I controlled our finances? You know what an absolute fuckwit she is, don't you? How many times since you've known her has she lost her bank cards? Or forgotten her PIN number? Or dropped her purse somewhere, never to be seen again? I had to organise all the bills, keep an eye on what went in and out of the joint account... and all this time she was stashing cash for herself anyway. She's un-fucking-believable.

I suddenly realised that if you'd been siphoning off cash to this savings account for all this time, you must have been planning to leave me for... how long? Even after everything we'd talked about in the summer, when you'd let me grovel and beg you to stay. Had you been planning this nonetheless all that time, going about our lives together as if nothing was wrong? I thought about it, and it blew my mind. The daily, routine intimacies that you'd been faking for months – maybe longer. The I love yous, the kisses and hearts on thousands, tens of thousands of texts exchanged. Sex, albeit less often, and more often than not in the same, predictable format. But these things were impossible to fake, weren't they? Were they? Had you lived a lie for so long, so expertly? Everything I thought we were was crumbling, finally, into dust.

There had been that one time. When I'd seen an email on your laptop, left lying on the sofa one evening late last summer. I knew the passwords that were needed to open it up because I'd set up a joint calendar for us years ago, which required being logged into your email account. Whenever you forgot the password, or locked yourself out – which was often – it was always me who'd had to sort it out for you. That day, when I logged in, I'd seen something at the top of your inbox that I didn't look away from. I knew I probably shouldn't read it, but I'd seen my name at the top and couldn't help myself. And I'd been so devastated to see your account of me, written to your fucking ex of all people, about how shit our life was. I'd told you so, and you'd brushed it off, saying it was my fault for prying. I could see now that it was an early version of the story you'd told your lawyer. Quite the narrator, you'd turned out to be.

I turned back to my phone, where Nancy was still holding the line. How dare she position herself as morally superior? I ranted. Did Nancy remember that time you said you'd had your bike stolen, and I'd stepped in to sort everything out with the police and the insurers, before realising it hadn't been stolen at all? You hadn't locked it up, you'd only looped your chain around a post but not the bike, and someone had just walked away with it. It was the kind of stupid shit you did all the time, that I had to sort out for you. Except that time I'd drawn the line at making a claim, and lying to the police, and had told you to clean up your own mess. What a spectacular fight that had started.

Nancy tried her best to be reasonable, to rationalise your irrationality. It only made me angrier. I explained that you'd already been looking at flats to move into. I actually remembered you looking, stopping in the street to browse the listings in estate agent windows as I stood right next to you. What kind of twisted fuck does that? And not any ordinary flats, not for you: nice big spacious Hackney flats.

And you'd also been kind enough to check out some shitty little studios around my office in Elephant, so that your lawyer could tell their own story about what I needed, and how much of that would be so generously financed by my tiny share of the flat, my own home, once it was sold.

I got louder and louder, shouting now without pausing for breath, gasping for air as I bellowed into my handset. Nancy shouted back, telling me to stop, to not take it out on her, to calm myself down. I couldn't. I didn't even want to. I knew she was going to hang up, and when she did I felt vindicated, stupidly triumphant in my isolation. Of course I'd be on my own in this shit show. Wasn't I always?

I stormed around the house, kicking things out of my way, throwing things into boxes. What a fucking mug. Feeling bad about this plan to move my things out, to give you the shock of arriving back to a ravaged home. That was nothing compared to what you were planning. You'd actually checked your mortgage capacity, and thought you knew what you had to spend on your new house. You utter cunt. I wouldn't be surprised if you'd already looked round a few, imagining yourself in your new life, me conveniently packed off to some shithole in south London.

And you'd found the perfect excuse for your greed: that you needed to be near your 'close network of friends and family' while you separated from this ogre that is me. That I was controlling and abusive. That you'd been so frightened of me you'd contacted a domestic violence helpline. Had you? What had you said? What had they said in reply?

I finished packing, finished moving furniture and cleaning and organising. I sat down in the stripped living room, and read the pages through again and again, countering what I read in order to keep straight in my head my version of events. Yours was so overwhelming.

It got later and later, and I remained hunched over them, typing notes into my phone so I'd remember why they were wrong. The more I went over them, the more scared I became. What would happen, now that you'd told this story? I heard a siren outside, and saw a blue light flashing against the walls of the house opposite. My heart stopped: they've come for me. You have told them all these things, and now they've come for me.

I waited for the police to knock on the door, but no sound came. I felt mad. I couldn't settle myself; I didn't know what was going to happen. Whatever it would be, I knew it wouldn't be good.

It was a long night. Eventually I went to bed, knowing the removals people would be arriving early. I lay awake, going over and over the things that I'd read. I had to be ahead of you now, had to make sure I didn't let you win. It calmed me a little bit when I thought: you're nowhere near as smart as you think you are. I can beat you at this game.

The men with their van were right on time, pulling up outside the flat at 7 a.m. It took them under an hour to load everything, and another three-quarters to take it all out again once we got to the storage depot. Two hours to deposit my life into a square box only just wider than my arm span. I was home before 10 a.m., and all that remained was to grab my overnight bag and head round to my friends'.

I was taking one last look around the place when I heard a noise downstairs. The front door onto the street had opened. I held my breath, and couldn't believe my ears when I heard the sound of a key being pushed into the lock in our front door.

You were here.

I had wished for this moment for weeks, and now I stood paralysed, not knowing what to do. My mind raced through what might now happen: had you come back to say you were sorry, to take back all those terrible lies? Were you ready to put all this behind us? Shit, all my stuff was now in storage – should I go back and get it?

I walked downstairs quietly. You were inside the hallway on the other side of our flat door. I took a breath, and pulled the door open just as you put your key to it. For a split second, you looked me right in the eye. Time froze. I believed, just for that instant, in the old you: the one I thought I'd fallen in love with. The one that was missing in action. The one I wanted back, more than anything else in the world. Then you dropped your gaze, and that image of you fell to the floor and smashed into a million tiny pieces.

You shouldn't be here. I told you I was coming back this morning and you shouldn't be here.

Lovely to see you too, darling. It's been a while, hasn't it? Have you missed me?

I may or may not have said this out loud. I honestly can't re-member now, it's all a blur. A blur of you turning on your heel, and marching back out of the hallway, dragging your wheely case furi-ously behind you. A blur of me following you out down the front path, calling after you to stop, to wait, to just fucking *listen* for a minute.

You'd got the day wrong: you were back at the flat twenty-four hours earlier than you'd said you would be after the Christmas break. How could you make that mistake if you really didn't want to see me? Surely some part of you wanted us to sit together, to talk. To be like we were. To be far away from what we had become.

I ran after you. I knew I shouldn't, but I'd waited so long, hoped so desperately, and I knew I had to make the most of this opportunity.

I thought that, deep down, you must have wanted me to.

Stop, just stop. STOP. How can you be like this? What's wrong with you? I just want to talk; it doesn't make sense to me that you won't speak to me. What have I done to make you be like this?

Won't you just fucking stop and talk to me? PLEASE?

I'm not sure how many streets I tailed you down. I couldn't help myself, I felt compelled to keep trying. To keep trying to reach you. I couldn't accept that this wasn't what you wanted me to do. Not really. This stupid, stubborn, childish part of me still believed you might care about me. And still wanted that, above all else – and certainly above any regard I might have for how ridiculous I was making myself. I noticed people staring, and I didn't care. I put everything I had into these final, desperate pleas.

And then I watched, numb, as you walked away.

And then I sat down on the ground, on the street, and I stayed there.

I had nowhere else to go.

It was after that I started behaving badly. I was only following your lead, after all. The fear that I'd felt reading those pages of lies morphed into something different, something meaner. I calmed down, became more calculating.

I began to take my petty revenges.

I became a thrill-seeker, chasing my kicks by breaking or stealing things of yours that I knew you'd be upset by. I wasn't reactive, and mad, as I had been when I'd thrown your things in anger. I was deliberate, and small, and horrible. I was like you.

It was a secret I kept from everyone: only you would know the truth, discovering the absences and the damage I wrought in time. My vengeance was served cold: I was happy to wait for you to be hurt by my childish torments.

So where you'd carefully placed a trio of plant pots, telling me authoritatively that interiors were all about the power of threes, I took one of them and left it on a wall by the train station, delighted by the idea that it would end up in a stranger's home by the end of the day. Or the street cleaner's cart. I wasn't fussed either way.

I became distracted by your oil painting on the wall in the living room, an investment you'd made before we met, convinced that the artist would one day be collectable, and you rich. I hoped fervently now that that would never happen, but I also toyed obsessively with the idea of some deliberate sabotage. What would the value of it be with a line gouged out of the textured surface of the paint? Or a slice cut into the canvas? I settled for pencilling in the word 'cunt' on the back, a subtle message that I hoped you'd enjoy reading when you finally moved out of the flat. Perhaps even before.

Looking back, I wish I'd used a Sharpie.

I did more. Not big things, just small annoyances to remind you that I existed, and to cast a pall over your day. I wanted you to feel just a shadow of the great big fucking cloud that had hung over me in the months since you'd left. I chucked away your phone charger, left by the bed one morning when you vacated the flat for the week, forgetting to unplug it before I came back that evening. I took some of your socks, a particularly natty pair, and kept them in a drawer at Zed's, a pathetic trophy. I snapped off a lipstick that I found in the bathroom cabinet, smearing its column of iridescent red over the mirror and then cleaning it, badly, in time for your return. I enjoyed imagining you irritated by these things. I was glad I had the power to get at you.

When you accidentally left behind a new coat – one that I noted via a furious Google search had cost you almost a grand – I wrestled with my conscience for the entire weekend about dropping it off at the local homeless shelter. It would have been a poetic, pyrrhic victory: calling out the dishonesty behind your lawyer's claims of your impoverishment and subsequent demand for a greater share of our joint assets, while debasing myself in a way that would reveal me more petty than even you.

Part of me still wishes I'd done it. Another part is satisfied that I left a small but annoying ink stain on the arm, after accidentally brushing past it with a leaky biro. Such reward in taking the moral high ground.

From: Me (NEW)
Subject: Fwd: Re: Big fat new start!
Date: 5 January at 18:38:17 BST
To: michelle.hendry@HendryPriceLLP.co.uk

Dear Michelle, you asked that I take some time to consider any further incidents in the chronology we started to set out when I first came to your office at last October.

I apologise that I didn't tell you about these events at our last meeting, but I wasn't ready then to talk about them with you. It has taken me a while to come to terms with what I've been through with J. You've been very kind and so I feel reassured that you will help me make sense of these events, and also help me set them out clearly in order to progress my legal case.

I've also forwarded an email I've just sent to my sister, which sets out some of what I wanted to tell you. The rest I haven't been able to tell my sister about, since it involves her directly – but I wanted you to know about it.

As well as the violence, which I've written about below, there were other things that slowly depleted me during my relationship with J. As you know, J controlled all aspects of our lives together, and I always felt that I had to do as I was told. There were times when I tried to stand up for myself, but J has a bad temper, and I would end up feeling too scared to stick to my guns.

Some of the things that happened sound silly now, but I want to spell them out as I think they help show how much J was in charge of me and wanted me to do as I was told.

One thing I remembered was when I changed the photo on my phone screen from a picture of J to one of me and my sister. I hadn't thought anything of it, I just really liked the pic: it was of the two of us on the beach near my mum's house, and it made me smile to look at it. But when J noticed that I'd swapped it, we had a massive row. J thought it meant I prioritised my sister over our relationship, which I thought was ridiculous, and accused me of not being romantic or caring. I remember feeling frightened by how upset J was, and in the end I just switched the old photo back. I can see now how much my self-esteem had been worn down, so I did what J wanted.

And J would constantly attack and undermine my sister, as I think the closeness of our relationship felt like a threat. J said my sister was a pain – she was too loud, too much of a show-off – and didn't like it when she came round with her family. It was all too false, J said, and never considered how that would make me feel. It drove a wedge between me and her.

J also made up a story about my sister's husband having an affair. J said that anyway it was OK that Tom cheated, saying you couldn't blame him for wanting some fun. It made me wonder what Tom and J had spoken about, and I was really worried for my sister. It also made me wonder if J was doing the same. I thought it was horrible that J didn't seem to care about how hurtful the whole thing was to my sister. And to me. I can see now that it was part of a bigger picture where J disparaged the things that I cared about, and tried to isolate me from my family. My family are everything to me, and for far too long I let J dictate how much I saw them, and when. I feel terrible about it now.

I hope these things don't seem silly to you. I only bring them up now as you were very clear I should document all the things that J did to control and manipulate me. I hope it's OK that I wrote to you today.

I look forward to our next meeting, and please remember to email me using this address, not my old one, as I'm worried that J might still be hacking it. I can't be sure that the password is secure on it.

Thanks for all your help so far.

Begin forwarded message:
From: Me (NEW)
Subject: Re: Big fat new start!
Date: 2 January at 15:02:25 BST
To: snapzzz187@gmail

Hello sis,

I got back to the flat today and guess what? J's emptied it.
Everything has gone. I told you something like this would happen,
didn't I? I knew it.

I've called my solicitor but there's no one there today. I left
a message on her voicemail so hopefully she'll get back to me.
Although I don't know what she'll be able to do to get my stuff
back now. God knows where J's put it all. I bet Nancy and Zed
helped out. I bet they all had a right laugh about it.

You know I started telling you something the night before
last, but then I stopped? Well, I want to tell you now. It's time I
stopped covering for J, and I know I can trust you to keep this to
yourself. I feel really ashamed. I don't want everyone knowing
what I've been dealing with.

You know that J has problems. I've told you about how controlled I've felt, and you've seen J lose it with me. Remember that
time when we went away for the weekend? How awful it was,
and you had that argument and J smashed a glass? I know you
thought you'd seen then how bad things could be, but you hadn't,
not really.

You were the first person who said you thought J was controlling and abusive. At the time I was really shocked because I
hadn't thought of using those words before. You were right, J
is really controlling, but no one else sees it. Everyone thinks I'm
really uptight and neurotic, and J has spent years making it look
like I'm a pain. And you too: everyone thinks you're too loud
and too annoying, because J has said these things about you and

people are seduced by how charming and fun and attentive they think J is.

J's always been mean about you. I've tried to keep it from you as I knew it would really upset you. But we've had loads of arguments about it. J has called you thick because you've got your words muddled or said something oppositional. I said it was outrageous, especially because of your dyslexia, to be so judgey and spiteful. That only ever made it worse. J's been mean about the way you talk, what you do, where you live… I've had to walk on eggshells the whole time we've been with you and Tom.

I'm telling you all this now because I want you to understand that I've been protecting you from the real J. And I'm not going to do it any more, I've had enough. At least if I tell you the truth, I'll feel a bit safer and I know you'll believe me, even if no one else does. I've tried to speak to a couple of our friends over the holidays about what's been going on, but no one wants to hear it.

The reality is that J is more than just controlling. The abuse isn't just the shouting and the put-downs. It's physical too. I haven't told you before because I was scared it would make things worse at home, I knew you'd want to say something. I didn't know if J would hurt you too.

It's only happened a few times, but I was scared of it becoming a habit, and that's why I had to leave. I should have spoken to you about it this week, and I nearly did, but it is just so huge a thing to open up. And I was freaked out anyway, because of J phoning you and Tom to try to get through to me. I thought that by blocking my number I would be able to create a bit of a safe space. I should have guessed J wouldn't care about dragging you both into it. I can't believe we had to spend so much time on New Year's Eve – which I'd been so looking forward to – dealing with J's madness. It was really good of Tom to answer, but I wish he hadn't. I don't want anyone else speaking to J any more – I don't trust what will be said. I don't want you to have to deal with it.

Anyway, I told my solicitor about the phone calls too, and

she's made a note. She says it's all part of the wider picture of J's abuse and I should keep a record of everything that happens, as we might need to produce evidence later on. You should do the same, actually, if J rings again. Make a note of the time and what is said, and the tone of voice, all that sort of stuff. My solicitor says that J's line at New Year, about not being responsible for what happens if I didn't take the call, is classic behaviour for an abuser. They find it very difficult to see that they're responsible for the things that go wrong in their lives, and when things begin to spiral the behaviour always gets worse. That's what's happening now.

I've told you about all this before, but I've never mentioned the physical stuff. So here goes…

It started pretty soon after we got married. It's as though being married meant that J could relax, let down the guard a bit. I was snagged, so there was no need to be on best behaviour any more. You know we've always argued, and you know J can be a bully. I've often felt completely overruled and ignored, and I've spoken to Mum about it a bit as well as you. She was worried, and said I should speak to you more but you're so busy and I knew you'd worry too.

At first it wasn't directed at me. It would start with door slamming and kicking furniture and stuff like that, which would frighten me. It was always so aggressive. But it only happened when J really lost it, if we'd had a big fight about something. Looking back now, I think it was all meant to make me feel scared, so that I'd back down. I never knew when it would happen, and I never knew where it would end.

Then something else happened and I started to see that we were in a really destructive pattern, that would start with J getting angry and end with something violent happening. We went for dinner at a friend's house, just after Christmas last year, and we had an argument when we got home which ended up with us sort of wrestling on the sofa and J pushing me really hard, gripping me on both shoulders and shoving me backwards. It was shocking. I remember thinking that there was a wild look in J's eyes, and I was scared. It felt like anything could happen, like J was really out of control.

We sort of laughed it off the next morning. J said we must have looked absolutely mad, scrapping like that, blamed it on too much alcohol and not enough sleep. I agreed. It just felt sort of ridiculous and I didn't really want to think about it again because I felt a bit ashamed. But I knew we'd stepped over a line, and I wanted to talk to someone else about it, to get someone else's perspective. I wish I had done, now.

Of course that wasn't the end of it at all. It kept on happening, J kept losing it, I kept on being scared. The punching was the worst. J would get really wound up, and say it was my fault that things got so heated. Do you remember that saying J used: that I could start an argument in an empty room? There was so much belittling like that. I hated it, and J would do it around our friends to make me look like the mad one. Not around you so much – although even with you and Tom, sometimes you all laughed along with it.

Anyway, there was one time I'd been out somewhere and I was a bit late back for dinner. J made a massive fuss about it, because I hadn't seen the messages and calls on my phone – I'd been round to Jane's to pick up a yoga mat that was going spare, and had got chatting. J went on and on about how I never put us first, I'd ruined dinner, I was so selfish, the usual ranting. I'd seen all the missed calls when I looked at my phone on the bus on the way home, so I'd been bracing myself for something from the minute I put my key in the front door. Sure enough, J stormed out of the kitchen, chucking food all over the place, and when I went upstairs a few minutes later to see if things had calmed down, I knew something bad was going to happen. J kept on shouting at me, and then suddenly came across the bedroom with a clenched fist, and punched the wall next to my head. I was scared shitless. I ran out of the room and told J to stay upstairs, I didn't want to be in the same room for the rest of the night. I slept on the sofa in the end, and then just went to work as if everything was normal in the morning. How awful is that? I didn't really know what else to do about it, and J just never mentioned it again, so I sort of let myself forget about it. It made me feel like I was losing myself, so I buried it.

And then all this year there have been more and more incidents where J has lashed out. Whenever we've had an argument J has done something threatening, like blocking my way out of a room or out of the flat. It's just got worse and worse. I should have said something to you ages ago but I didn't really have the will. I feel broken.

When I got back today there was blood on the floor in the kitchen. God knows how it got there, but I think J left it there deliberately, as a warning. I'm really worried now that things will get out of control, and so I wanted to tell you everything, write it all down, so that you understand what J is like. And so that there's a record of it in case anything really bad does happen to me.

I don't think you've ever understood who J is. I don't think anyone has, except me. I'm not going to keep this horrible secret any more. Being honest about it now will help me get my head straight and get out of this mess in one piece.

Thanks, sis, let's talk it over on the phone once you're back in later on. There's lots more I can tell you and I want to explain what it all means in terms of the divorce and the flat and everything. You're a massive help, I love you loads. Thanks for being there for me. And thanks for having me over for Christmas and New Year. It was fun, wasn't it?

Talk to you in a bit. Love ya xxxx

On 2 Jan, at 09:34, <snapzzz187@gmail.com> wrote:

Hello, sis, hope you get home OK and everything's all right when you get there. Thanks for a tip-top Christmas and New

Year – so much more fun without J! You made the right decision you know.

I know it's tough but you've got to just think of yourself from now on. You're single now, put yourself first. J just wasn't right for you, it's no one's fault – definitely not yours.

Let me know if you need anything. I'll do anything to help you get what you want out of this. You deserve it.

Love ya xxxxx

February

I was going to turn forty at the end of the month. A terrible thought. My mind wandered frequently to the many milestone birthdays I'd been involved in organising: the bands, the speeches, the long long nights of consumption and the subsequent days in recovery that followed. I loved a good party. You were always more reticent, often disparaging the behaviour of the crowd: too reckless, too indulgent, too *old*. The idea of celebrating my own mid-life was laughable: what the fuck would I be celebrating? I'd lost my marriage, my home; I was feeling estranged from friends; most days I felt pretty close to losing my mind, and to top all of it off: the fucking cat ran away.

I think I'd half expected it. I'd thought about what to do with him during those dark few days when I was packing up the flat. I didn't trust you not to steal him, to install him in someone else's house – your sister's, most likely – and to tell me I wasn't getting him back.

I wasn't going to let that happen.

He was the most beautiful little animal. We'd collected him from the boot of a hatchback in a car park in Stratford, under cover of darkness one winter's evening. We'd laughed about the sordid pick-up plan, the black marketeering: it felt like we were collecting a firearm, or a human organ. Not a tiny harmless ball of ginger fur.

The breeder assured us that he'd had a good start in life, staying with his mother and siblings until he was handed over to us. He fitted neatly in the palm of my hand. I loved him immediately. We gave him a tough name so he wouldn't be a victim to the other, rough neighbourhood cats. We thought Rambo was hilarious. Remember when we made jokes like that together?

I loved those first few months with him, when we were still living in my old flat. When I wasn't in my office on campus, he would badger me while I tried to work at home, sitting on my knee while I sat at the computer. More problematically, sitting on my keyboard.

He was the most affectionate animal I'd ever met. He kept us awake night after night, crawling onto our faces to sleep or trying to burrow under our bodies, getting as close as he could. We'd shut him out of the bedroom, but he'd shunt his tiny body against the door for hours, trying to be let back in. Eventually we devised an elaborate bedtime routine, locking him downstairs in the kitchen with pillows pulled back against the door as we closed it behind us: there to both muffle the sound of him hurling himself against it, and to mitigate against him hurting himself in the process.

He was always desperate to be as close to me as he could.

What a contrast to you.

I could tell, these last few weeks, that he was really unhappy. I'd said so to Zed, sounding stupid even to myself: I think the cat is depressed. I had a nagging feeling that something was going to happen with him. He hated being on his own for long periods of time, and I had no idea what happened to him on the days you had possession of the flat. When I had it, I barely went out, and we would huddle together under the duvet while I mainlined boxsets on my laptop.

And then one day, he wasn't there. I got in from work, and I knew straight away that he'd gone. I didn't blame him. It was fucking horrible coming back to that stripped-out space. Even he knew it. I went out into the street and walked slowly up and down, calling out to him. I heard nothing. I knocked on doors and spoke to people I vaguely recognised, and some I'd never seen before. In the morning I did it again, then went to work to make flyers and buy tape so I could paste them across the neighbourhood. I was furious with you for taking yet another thing from me. One less thing now anchored me to my former life. I wondered if you'd taken him, and realised I wouldn't put anything past you. But somehow I knew he'd just wandered off by himself. I was devastated not to even get a goodbye.

I knew you'd be upset he was gone, and that pleased me. I wanted you to be in pain. If it wasn't because of me – and you'd made it crystal clear it wasn't – then well done little cat for penetrating your icy fucking exterior. Either way, I'd never know. I hadn't heard from you in weeks. Not even your lawyers had been in touch.

The cat's departure helped me make my mind up about my birthday. Since I didn't need to be back at the flat now for him – and being there was so depressing I tried to avoid it even while insisting on my rightful days of occupation – I decided I would go away. Far away. Away from all this chaos and the shredded life I was now trying to live. And on my own. I was really tired of making the effort to talk to people, to try to help them understand what was happening when I did not. Your behaviour was so extreme, so shocking, that it wasn't only me that was struggling. I'd had to explain over and over to my friends and family that you wouldn't talk to me, you were going through lawyers, and I didn't know why. I'd held my tongue as they mulled over the reasons, biting back the fucking obvious: you were damaged, and you were damaging, and it was simply my turn.

I considered my options. Somewhere hot, that was a no-brainer. The endless grey days in London were making everything feel worse. I thought about the places we'd said we'd go to together, plans we'd sketched out over long Sunday mornings in bed. I faltered. Could I really do this on my own? How miserable would I be making a trip of a lifetime when my own life was in tatters?

Then I considered how annoyed you'd be if I did, and it spurred me on. I had the freedom to do this, while you were tied to your job. I knew I'd be able to take as much time off as I needed – my boss had said so, and was pushing for me to do it. Why look a gift horse in the mouth? Get away for a bit, and revel in the contrast between your shitty life and mine.

So I chose Cambodia. I announced my plans to Nancy and Zed over dinner, a couple of weeks before my birthday. They'd arranged to take me out so they could check in on me, and check that the plans they were making for my party were OK. It was fun to watch them as they took in my news. A mixture of panic and encouragement, like a parent observing their child's first attempt to ride a bike. Are you sure that's a good idea? It's a really long way away if you realise you're not going to be OK on your own, you know?

I knew. But I wasn't OK on my own now. It didn't really matter where I was in the world, I hadn't been OK for a long time. I had better just get used to it.

I want to go somewhere where I can consider my insignificance in an infinite universe, I announced. If I'm immersed in an ancient culture that's lasted through millennia, how can I still think that what's happening to me is so bad? And at least I'll have the sun on my face, and the beer is cheap – and I can't bear to be here for my birthday. At this, my voice cracked, and I knew I'd won the argument.

Zed and Nancy understood, I think. They knew I'd been dreading my birthday, and I suspect they also thought that having a party for the world's most miserable forty-year-old would be a bit of a downer. They made a half-hearted effort to talk me out of it, but by the end of the night I knew I was going to do it. And so did they.

At work the next morning I started making proper arrangements. My colleagues thought it was a great idea, and those of them that had heard about what was happening with us told me it was the best thing I could do. Get away from her and her controlling bullshit, they said. Give yourself a good time. None of them knew you, they'd met you only a couple of times, so it was really easy for them to position you as the arsehole. I gladly let them. It was nice not to worry about nuance.

One of the interns said she'd been planning to visit Cambodia too, part of a bigger trip she was taking around Vietnam, Laos and

Thailand. She asked what dates I'd be there and, feeling momentarily enthusiastic and upbeat, I told her and said we should hook up if our plans overlapped. She was keen, but by the time I left the office that evening, I really hoped she'd change her mind.

There wasn't much time to arrange everything. Zed had a friend who lived near Siem Reap, and told me to just sort out my flights, and they'd come up with a plan for my accommodation. Then I got an email from Briony – a friendship you'd always been jealous of – who told me she had booked me in for two nights at the Foreign Correspondents' Club in Phnom Penh: a soft landing while I got my head around the rest of my plans. I replied with a half-hearted refusal – it was too expensive, too generous – but was glad when she insisted. I knew it was good that the first part of the trip was sorted: I was a bit overwhelmed by the idea of going away. I didn't know what you would do in my absence. I didn't want to relinquish what little control you'd left me, so I insisted no one talk about what I was planning. You weren't speaking to me, but there were people that we both knew who you must be seeing. I was really clear with my friends: don't tell her. I don't want her to fuck this up for me.

At the end of the week, Briony insisted I go round for dinner, a final farewell to me, and to my thirties. My flight was leaving at the start of the following week. It had all come round really quickly.

Zed answered the door when I got to Briony's and led me through to the kitchen. There was my gang of four, my best friends: Nancy and Zed and Briony and Gav. I hadn't seen much of them since you'd left, and it was good, really good, to see them now. I'd forgotten how much I loved to entertain, to command an audience, crack jokes, play the clown. I settled in with a drink and let myself be fussed over, fed. These were my people and they'd been in my life since long before you were, and would be long after this was all over.

We ate dinner, and avoided talk of you. They laughed about my impending middle age, my mission to find myself by traipsing out east. I repeated my line about considering my insignificance in an infinite universe, to howls of laughter. It cheered me right up.

After the food was cleared away, there was a sudden burst of activity, manic whispering in the corner and smiling glances in my direction. I pretended not to notice as a glow of candlelight appeared from under the kitchen counter, and then laughed as a cake only just large enough to fit forty candles onto was brought over to me, singeing the hairs on my arms as it was passed onto the table.

I blew the fire out and cut slices of the cake. Zed stood up and I got ready for more piss-taking, further references to my age or my maturity or my lack thereof.

Instead, Zed produced a large white envelope and passed it over, saying only that it was a gift from the group. Not only the ones in the room, but all our friends, who loved me and wanted me to have a happy birthday. Even though they all knew how hard that would be.

I opened the envelope and pulled out a homemade card, a Zed Photoshop special. On the front I sat resplendent in a rickshaw and blonde wig, an image of my head transposed from some late-night party some time, somewhere. And there lining the street were all my friends in similar states of disarray, cropped cleverly from other images and dropped into this bizarre scene that merged decadence with squalor in a perfect evocation of the trip I was about to undertake. I laughed, a lot. And then I opened the card, and it slowly dawned on me what this was all about. They'd all chipped in, every one of them, to pay for a hotel near the temples of Angkor Wat, as well as a driver and some spending money for when I got there. I was really moved, and worried I would show it. I tried to say thank you, but stopped myself as my voice wobbled. I flashed a thumbs up instead, and looked down at the floor.

There was a quiet pause, and then Zed got hold of me in a hug and told me to pull myself together. I couldn't get the words out to say thank you, at first, and then I couldn't say anything else. Just repeated myself over and over, eventually deciding to simply shut up and sit down, and carry on drinking. Safer that way; I was less likely to embarrass myself further. But I remember thinking I was really, honestly grateful to have friends like these. It was the proof I needed that I could draw people to me, I could be liked. Loved, even. I wasn't such a piece of shit after all. In spite of what you said.

I got to the airport before sunrise the following Tuesday, the birthday card packed in my bag along with mosquito spray, sunscreen and a minimal amount of clothing. I'd also packed three empty notebooks, believing I would spend my time writing, putting myself back together by jotting down what you had done, and what was left to do. I wanted to make the most of my time away to get ready for what would happen when I got back.

I landed first in Kuala Lumpur, almost a full day after taking off. I felt miserable. I had watched film after film during the flight, taking a break to eat the food that was put in front of me every four hours or so, failing dismally to fall asleep in between. I wanted to go home. I wanted to be back in our bed, in our flat, in our old lives. I didn't want what I was setting out for: adventure and solitude and answering only to myself. What the fuck had I been thinking?

Waiting for my connection, I tried to sleep on a bench in KL airport, my bag under my head, my legs curled up as best I could manage. Exhausted, I drifted off for an hour and then panicked about missing the flight, running down to the gate in a frenzy only to sit there for another ninety minutes until finally boarding. When I landed in Phnom Penh everything seemed too much, and I faltered again when I realised no one was waiting for me at arrivals, ready to whisk me to my room at the Foreign Correspondents' Club. I found out later that the car, arranged and paid for by Briony, had in fact arrived but I had been late, and they'd departed without me. They'd even come back an hour later, but by then I'd bundled myself into a taxi and arrived at the hotel on the riverfront, gratefully paying my driver a ludicrous tip on top of his fare before being shown up to my room by the bellboy.

Inside, I'd immediately taken off my clothes in response to the sticky heat of the city. Standing just in my underwear, there had been a knock on the door and before I could move to answer it, the same bellboy opened it and stepped inside, holding a plate in his hand. I stood absolutely still, turning crimson as he smirked at me and put the plate on a table to the side of the door. A birthday cake for you, he said. Happy birthday.

I turned the lock on the door behind him and threw myself onto the bed. Ten minutes in this city, and I'd already flashed a bellboy. I smiled to myself, and thought about how much everyone would laugh when I told this story back at home. The thought made me sad again. I had to pull myself together or this trip was going to be a total waste of time.

I decided to run a bath, and then head out into the late afternoon to get my bearings, and get a drink. My phone sat on the side of the tub as I lay in the cool water, the heat of the room hovering above the surface. There were messages from Nancy, and Zed, and my mum of course. My sister too. And then, as I read through them, one popped up from the intern, checking to see if I was still going to be in Phnom Penh this week. Fuck. I'd forgotten about her. The last thing I wanted was to entertain some twenty-something-year-old while I was supposed to be spending time alone, being contemplative, thinking big thoughts.

I knew that I had engineered the situation. I'd given her enough encouragement to think I'd be glad to see her, but not enough to make it an expectation. I was doing it to hurt you. It wasn't sophisticated, or clever, and I was pretty fucking certain it wouldn't be effective. You'd never even know it had happened. And if you did, you wouldn't care. It wouldn't penetrate that icy rock in your chest, not now.

I headed out of my hotel and into the heat of a Cambodian afternoon. Everything was blindingly bright, searingly hot, strange and unfamiliar. But it was exciting, too, I had to admit that. There's always something thrilling about arriving somewhere new, and so totally different to home.

I walked along the river, comparing it favourably to the grey waters of the Thames. There were traditional fishing boats bobbing on the water, street vendors doling out plastic bags of fried insects, children playing Frisbee and football on the grassy stretches between the water and the road. For the first time in a long time, I relaxed, a little. It was good to be away from home, from the mess you'd made of me. I walked round the city for an hour or two, smiling at the food van with a 'Pizza Express' sign, the hoarding advertising the Brighton International School for Languages. I decided to eat on the verandah at my hotel, and took a photo of my meal, documentation of my brave adventure. I added a second beer to the one I'd photographed, and was glad to finally feel ready for sleep. Within minutes of getting, gratefully, in between the white sheets of my bed, I was flat out.

In the morning I took Zed's advice. 'Perhaps a cheery afternoon at the Choeung Ek Genocidal Center may help put things into perspective?' I took a bus out of town, and wondered at the bustling tourist industry that had grown out of this darkest part of the country's history. Cambodia's killing fields. I passed through the gate into a large garden, at the centre of which was a white memorial. The gardens surrounding it were quiet, and quite beautiful. Butterflies batted over the uneven grass, and I walked around the perimeter, taking in the many signs that described what had happened there. It was so distant, inconceivable now, in this calm quiet. At the back of the gardens, people were at work in a rice field, knee-deep in water, bent low to their task. Everything was strange. I felt like an alien, newly landed on a foreign planet. Sadness overwhelmed me, and again, I considered my loneliness, feeling deeply, painfully sorry for myself.

So much for getting some perspective.

I turned back towards the entrance and tried not to laugh at a sign that read: 'Please don't walk through the mass grave!' I imagined you laughing at this too. You'd always shared my feelings about misplaced exclamation marks.

It was strange to come out, past the mausoleum housing thousands of human skulls, into the bustling marketplace where the bus was waiting to take me back to the city. Santa Bae Bae T-shirts were lined up alongside mementoes of the gardens; the juxtaposition was awful, but also darkly comic. There's money to be made, even at a site of genocide. What a mark of human endeavour.

I checked my phone when I got back to the hotel, and saw the intern had messaged me. She had arrived in the city, and was wondering if I was up for a drink. Knowing that I was playing with fire, I told her to come over, and then sat anxiously in the bar, asking myself what the fuck I was playing at. As if I didn't know.

She arrived quickly, and I realised she had come directly from the airport. I felt a jolt of panic: I didn't want to spend my trip with this woman, that was not the plan. The point of me being here was to do this by myself; the last thing I wanted was a hanger-on.

We ordered two cold lagers and sat down together, our table giving us a view of the river and the busy street below. Conversation was easy, which was a relief. We exchanged accounts of our journeys, and I set out my plans for the next two weeks, emphasising my decision to be here alone.

Subtle.

I told her about the killing fields, and showed her a photo of the sign that had made me laugh. She laughed too – another relief. I suppose it was a test, making sure she had the same kind of humour as you did. I would do that a lot, as the evening wore on.

We ordered refills of our drinks, once, twice, three times. We discovered a pool table in the back bar, where I showed off my skills and remembered how much you'd loved to watch me play. How you'd slide your hand up my T-shirt to distract me when I was taking a shot. That time we'd been in a pub by the seaside and you'd challenged a local to a game on my behalf. I'd been so relieved to win and then, later, delighted by your pride in me as we'd walked home along the beach.

The barman at the hotel was judging us, I could tell. Drunk Brits, the usual cliché. I agreed with him, and thought it best we head out for a bit. Get some food, try to sober up, get my head around what was happening. I was pretty certain there was an offer on the table for me. I just wasn't sure whether or not to take it.

We found somewhere nearby that served us up some noodles, which helped sober me up, just a little. We paid the bill and, standing outside the restaurant, I knew the moment had come to make a decision. I was caught between a terror of taking the intern back to the hotel, and dread of the rejection if I made a move and she said no.

Fuck it, I thought.

Fancy another? She didn't say no, and so we walked, almost in silence, back to where we'd come from. I let her into my room, thinking about you while smiling rigidly at her, and closed the door behind me, remembering to lock it against the risk of bellboy intrusions.

She was quick to kiss me, and at first I was pleased by how different it felt from you. Incredibly, my body remembered exactly what to do. It surprised me, as I had put all thoughts of sex completely out of my mind since you'd gone. I had zero interest in it. It was strange to feel myself go through the same motions as I always had, undressing this woman, kissing her, feeling her skin and her body against mine. I knew I was absolutely disengaged from her: while my hands and my mouth did their own thing, my mind was somewhere else, observing the action from a distance. I didn't feel very proud of myself. But I also didn't care. I wanted to feel intimacy, to feel desired. It didn't matter to me that I felt nothing, at all, in return.

In the morning, I woke up before sunrise, and lay perfectly still. I wasn't sure how things were going to go with the intern, and I didn't want to wake her to find out. I was filled with regret, wishing I could take back what I'd done. It was a step further towards us ending, and I didn't want it.

I just wanted this other flesh-and-bone woman to leave, so I could focus on the you that was inside my head.

She woke up around 7 a.m. and hurled herself out of bed and into the bathroom, emptying her bowels loudly, every emission audible through the flimsy screen door separating us. I was appalled, which felt churlish given what we'd done the night before.

She came back into bed and said how much her head hurt, before complimenting me on my performance the previous evening. I must have looked worried, because she laughed and said 'at the pool table' and it helped cut through some of the awkwardness. She told me she was on antidepressants, and it made it hard for her to come, and I tried to act cool and not show that I was slightly shocked by her talking so candidly. Fucking millennials.

I felt incredibly middle-aged. And I had nothing to say to her, not really, so I kissed her instead and repeated some of my moves from the night before. It was easier than talking.

My two nights in the hotel were up, and I had to catch my bus to Siem Reap for the next part of my trip. The intern said she was going that way too, and maybe because of the hangover, or the sex, or a combination of the two, I didn't want to be on my own again. I told her we should go together. I had a beautiful hotel sorted for me when I got there, courtesy of my amazing friends, and she might as well share it with me, at least for a night or two.

I am such a fucking idiot.

We checked out of my room, ignoring the looks of the staff who'd watched us stagger out and back in the night before. It was a short, hot walk to the bus station, where we could catch a ride all the way up the country to Siem Reap, the gateway to the Angkor ruins that I'd set my heart on seeing. It was the day before my birthday. I realised the date, and I wanted you to know what I'd been doing. I wanted to tell you and say I was sorry and see if you'd let me make it up to you. I knew none of this would ever happen, and I felt lost. It all fell away from me again.

We boarded the bus and I pretended to fall asleep almost straight away. I was behaving like a total shit, but I couldn't deal with having her there. I felt a kind of pressure creeping in at me from all sides, a desire to push her away.

The intern didn't try to engage me after that. In fact, she was dealing with me pretty well, all things considered. She knew I was separating from you, and she'd asked me about you a couple of times but been smart enough not to push it. It wasn't long before I actually did sleep, and I was glad to finally get some rest.

There was a driver waiting for me at the depot as the bus pulled in to Siem Reap's main terminal: actually a tiny shopfront by the side of the road. I waved to him, and watched as the intern dumped her bags in the boot next to mine. The driver had obviously been told to expect only one passenger, but he was very polite about it.

We arrived at the hotel, a low villa with a handful of beautiful huts arranged around its central pool. We were shown into my room, where gauzy curtains blew open onto a four-poster bed and lots of white linen. I deeply regretted being in company. It was a room set up for couples, and I was desperate to be alone in it.

But the next day I turned forty, and I couldn't face the thought of doing that by myself. It was too sad. So I smiled at the intern as the driver informed me that a massage had been arranged for me – and my friend – that evening in my room, a gift from my friends at home. I thought about that, wryly. I was pretty sure they hadn't imagined I'd have company.

I said I needed a bit of time to myself and the intern was more than happy to decamp to one of the cabanas lining the pool. I watched her as she plugged headphones into her phone and laid back, and was envious of her ability to be relaxed, be totally at peace in the place. I was also vaguely repelled by the way she'd flung her limbs across the pillows, the space she took up. I knew I was comparing her to you, and that she couldn't win. And I knew I was projecting my own shame onto her. I felt bad about it… but I felt it, nonetheless.

A couple of hours later, two stocky women, one young and one older, came into the room. I called across to the poolside and the intern joined me on the double bed, where we'd been indicated to lie down. Stripped to our underwear, we lay back as they got to work on our bare legs and arms, using the heat from their hands rather than oils or lotions as emollients.

I closed my eyes and went through a list of all the things I could say to the intern that would let her down gently, but ensure she would go. I had created a problem for myself that seemed too difficult to fix. I'd lost the ability to work out solutions. I felt ashamed of myself, and also desperate to be rid of her. It was the least relaxing massage I'd ever had.

After half an hour or so the women finished their work, standing up wordlessly and leaving the room. I stood up quickly and said I was going for a walk, grabbing my phone and some money and hurrying out of the room. I knew I was behaving like an arsehole. I just didn't care.

I walked around the town as the sun went down, glad to be on my own, worrying about how to keep it that way. Everything I looked at reminded me of you. Stupid things, like cafés that I knew you'd love to slip inside of, ordering your usual super-strength coffee with the milk on the side, so you could measure out exactly the right amount. There was bougainvillea growing along the roadsides, and I thought about our honeymoon, the bright pink flowers that had lined the walls along the path outside our tiny rental flat, where we'd walked down to a private beach to swim naked. It made me feel wretched. I trudged back towards the hotel, berating myself for failing so spectacularly to put you from my mind. You were everywhere. It was exhausting. But I didn't want to let you go.

I thought about turning forty the next day, and remembered the first time we'd celebrated my birthday. Mine was the first of our birthdays we'd been together for, and I had been overwhelmed by the effort you'd made for me. In the morning, over a long breakfast, we had lolled under the duvet as you produced one beautifully wrapped box after another from underneath the bed. I remembered, vividly, how happy we'd been that morning, the weak winter sun pouring in on us in our chaos of torn paper and spilled food. You had enjoyed, almost as much as me, the new clothes you had put me in, not taking your eyes off me when I got up, finally, to dress. You told me how gorgeous I was. And you took me out for lunch, walking with your arm tightly tucked around my waist, holding me in against the cold weather. Against the outside world. It was just me and you, strolling around the East End with eyes only for one another. It was perfect.

It's hard to remember cold weather when you're in a hot climate. It's hard to recall the feelings, the sensation of an icy blast of air when you're covered in a thin film of your own sweat. But I could feel it, then, the chill on my cheeks that day as I thought back to how we were. Six years less one day ago, wrapped up in you as we made our way through London together.

My birthday walk had ended at a boutique hotel in Shoreditch, where I'd followed you in feeling bewildered and then smiled, wider and wider, as you'd checked us in and I realised why we were there. I hadn't known you'd been in cahoots with Zed and Nancy, and that all my friends were waiting in the bar behind the reception, the one you entered via a secret knock, ducking down to slip into the other-worldly speakeasy beyond. It had turned into a raucous, indulgent and very, very long night. It, too, was perfect.

You'd made the day magical. I was absolutely and utterly under your spell.

I got back to my room to find the intern sprawled on the bed, still plugged into her phone. Let's get some dinner, I said. More a statement than a suggestion, but she was pliant enough, and we found somewhere not-too-touristy to eat where I paid for the food to allay my guilt at treating her so shittily. When we got back to the room, I said I was exhausted and went straight to bed, praying she'd get the hint. She did. She stayed by the pool for an hour or so then slipped in beside me, keeping a safe distance. By then, it was my birthday. I was forty. What a tragic fucking start to middle age.

I slept off and on until around 5 a.m., then got up and dressed and went out, pacing up and down streets, wallowing in my misery. I hoped that you'd contact me. I yearned for it. I was seven hours ahead of UK time so you'd have until tomorrow, Cambodian time, to send me a message. Just a text. It was inconceivable that I wouldn't hear from you on this day, when we'd spent so long talking about what we'd do when I finally hit the big four-o.

It had saved you a pile of money, leaving me, I thought drily. No need for presents, or parties, or a trip somewhere spectacular. But I'd never wanted any of that. This year, I just wanted to hear your voice. It was the only thing I wanted.

I was due to meet another driver at 9 a.m. who would take me up to Kbal Spean, a sacred riverbed into which hundreds of figures had been carved, millennia ago. I got back to the hotel room and forced a smile at the intern, who asked if she could join me on the trip. I couldn't think of any reason to say no so, silently cursing my own lack of imagination, I nodded and headed back to the car.

We drove out of town and up towards the jungle. I laughed as the driver explained that Kbal Spean had been a secret until only fifty years earlier, when a French ethnologist had been led up to the site by a local hermit. I found the image of that exchange hilarious. I imagined talking to you about it, making you laugh by picturing the scene. Why did the hermit decide to share his secret? How did the ethnologist find the hermit? Isn't that the point of hermits? That you don't know where they live?

When we reached the car park where we'd start the trek up to the riverbed, the intern handed me a small, wrapped parcel and wished me a happy birthday. I was touched, and taken aback. As I unwrapped the book she'd chosen for me, I told myself to stop behaving like an arsehole, and be nice. It wasn't her fault that all I could think of was you.

But it was harder than I thought. I wasn't at my best when I felt obliged to be in someone's company, when I felt crowded in. I knew I'd made it happen, I'd invited her to join me. I was selfish and arrogant and needy, and I was using her to make me feel a tiny bit less lonely, and sad. I had to sort myself out, and I had to let her down gently. I had to grow up a bit. It was time I started acting my (considerable) age.

It struck me how stupid I was being. I was at an ancient and beautiful site of archeological wonder, worrying about a one-night stand. I was ridiculous. I forced myself to smile at the intern, and thank her for my book, and fall into step beside her as we began the steep trek up through the jungle. I told myself to look forward to the evening, when we could drink and it would feel easier. To stop being so selfish, just for a little while.

It was an incredible place. After we'd walked up to get above the curve of the river, we followed it back down slowly, spotting the intricately carved scenes that sat below the surface of the water as well as in the rock face on either side. I concentrated on taking photographs, using it as an excuse to wander off and explore. Butterflies darted around above my head, and there were frogs and lizards blinking their way in and out of the river. It was magical. I was delighted to take it all in, and even more pleased when the intern vanished from view, leaving me in my own company. I resolved to be clear with her about going our separate ways as soon as possible.

I'd completely lost her by the time I made it back down to the car park, where I was courted by a number of stall-holders keen to sell me their fabrics and carved miniature deities. I thought about buying you one, fantasising about coming home to you, from this trip, telling you all about my adventures.

Well, most of them.

I sat under the tarp by the drinks vendor and let the daydream play out until the intern appeared, bursting my bubble. Where did you go, she said. I shrugged. I didn't realise she'd been looking for me. Sorry, I think I must have wandered off. Shall we get out of here?

We were driven on to a temple, Banteay Srei, which the driver told us was dedicated to the Hindu god Shiva, adding that he'd wait in the car until we were done looking round. It was hard to take it all in. Red sandstone walls and sculptures rose from the ground in a riot of patterns and shapes. It was so intricate and beautiful. More than a thousand years old, surviving not only nature's but humankind's assaults on it. It was the evidence I'd been looking for of my own insignificance, of the inexorable progression of time, of things greater and more permanent than my tiny, stupid, heartbroken reality. I went my own way, weaving in and out, smiling. I'd found, fleetingly, the distraction I was looking for.

When we got back to the hotel, I forced myself to have an adult conversation with the intern. I tried not to show that I was desperate to get rid of her. I asked her what her plans were for the next part of her trip, and felt huge relief that she got the hint. She said she was going to head off the next afternoon, after seeing Angkor Wat. Maybe we could go together the next morning and then she'd leave me to it?

I said yes, very quickly, feeling a bit giddy that it had gone so well. It meant I could relax into the evening – my birthday – and not worry about any awkward let-downs on my part. I was suddenly much cheerier. I told her to get ready to go out, it was time to start celebrating.

We went down to Siem Reap's main strip, and found a bar with a pool on the terrace, where we drank a couple of beers and watched the sunset. I had messages to respond to from people back at home, sending me love, imagining me alone as I saw in my fifth decade. I didn't disillusion them.

We went for dinner when it got dark, and I was touched that the intern had arranged for the restaurant to bring me a special dessert, my name written in chocolate sauce across the plate, flowers and sparklers adorning the cake. I didn't deserve it, I knew that. It was almost overwhelming to have someone do something so thoughtful for me. I was really touched. I was also really quite drunk.

Determined not to do anything stupid again, I suggested we call it a night pretty early. We went back to the hotel and I took myself straight to bed again. In the close confines of the room, I felt suffocated; desperate, again, to be on my own. It wouldn't be long now, I reminded myself.

I woke up around 4 a.m., the usual jolt into reality. I didn't want to be around when the intern woke up, and in spite of what I'd said the night before, I didn't think I could do another day with her. It took all of my energy to act like I wasn't falling apart and I had run out of steam.

An idea popped into my mind and as soon as I'd thought it, I knew I was going to do it. It was horrible of me, but I was delighted by it. I got out of bed and got dressed as quietly as I could, grabbing my camera and wallet and sneaking out of the room like a burglar, anxious not to make any noise.

I got out to the road and hailed a tuk-tuk, instructing the driver to take me to Angkor Wat. I was going to watch the sun rise at the temple. Alone. I didn't care that I'd promised to go later that day. As the tuk-tuk picked up speed I felt euphoric, free. I was escaping a confinement of my own making, and I was being a total bastard. It felt fantastic.

The driver stopped, indicating that I was to get out. There were a few other people ahead of me, and I started following them into the darkness. I couldn't see a thing, and was glad that they'd had the foresight to bring their phones, using them to light the path ahead. I got to a lake, where vendors were selling coffee and pastries, but I wanted neither. I walked round the shoreline to find a spot away from the small gangs of people already in place, waiting. It was surreal. I could just about make out some tall trees on the other side of the water, and felt irritated that I would have such a poor view of the temple, with them blocking my way. I tried to work out where else I could go, but it seemed that this was the vantage point everyone was sticking to. I decided to trust the crowd, and settled into position, watching the moon set, waiting for the sun to rise in its place.

When it did, I slowly realised that the trees I'd been so annoyed by were actually the temple I'd come to see. As the sun inched its way up over the horizon, these magnificent sandstone monuments came into relief, bulbous turrets rising above the walls beneath them. There was a collective murmur of delight as the pinks and blues of the sky became reflected in the water in front of me. I turned around to see how many were enjoying the same view, and blinked in disbelief: hundreds of people stood behind and beside me, hugging the shore of the lake and lined back as far as I could see. It was a crazy moment. I'd been engrossed in the sunrise, assuming myself to be among a small group of pilgrims, a tiny few that had made it here so early in the day. It made me laugh out loud to see how wrong I was.

I spent a while longer watching the light take over the sky. To my right side, a teenager was filming her reaction to the spectacle. She'll be so glad to look back on that in twenty years' time, I thought. The wonder of Angkor Wat, visible as a blurry backdrop to her grinning face.

I walked away from the lake and into the ruins of the temple, veering away from people as much as I could. It was impossible at first, but as I moved from Angkor Wat out to the temples of Ta Prohm and then Angkor Thom, it was easier to find my way out of the crowds. At the last of these ruins, Preah Khan, I found myself suddenly unable to continue. I could not stop thinking about you, and the mess we'd made of our marriage, and a sadness that felt profound and absolute descended. I couldn't walk any further. I peeled off the path to sit among the stones, away from the tourists and the locals. And there, finally still, I began to cry. I sobbed. It felt like it was beyond my control, a weeping that flowed out of me, unendingly. I couldn't stop it, and I didn't want to: I sat among those ancient stones and let the pain and fear and regret pour out.

I was there for a long time. Finally, I decided I had to get myself together. I considered my situation: I was alone among the ruins of a temple more than a thousand years old, and I was crying over a woman. For fuck's sake. Life had to be about more than this.

When I got back to the hotel that afternoon, the intern had gone, leaving me a terse message saying she'd headed out of town, via the temples, and would maybe see me back at Phnom Penh before I flew home. I knew that was not going to happen.

I took a seat by the pool, taking a beer with me from the fridge in my room. I felt pleased with myself. I'd been enough of a shit that, finally, I'd been left alone. I wanted to think about you, without distraction. I wanted to know why you hadn't even sent me one miserable message on the occasion of my fortieth birthday. Would that really have been too much for you?

I felt a now-familiar anger rise in my chest. I went to collect my phone from beside the bed, deciding that I was going to make contact with you, right now, no matter how long it took. I had your work mobile – you hadn't blocked me on that – and so I dialled the number, over and over again. Then I texted: I told you that I was away, and when I got back I was going to stay in the flat again, that we could share the space while we worked things out. I was sick of living out of a bag and we owed it to each other to end things better than this. Then I dialled again.

You picked up. I couldn't believe it.

Hello? It's me, I said.

I know. What do you want?

The tight anger in your voice was so familiar.

I wanted to speak to you because something significant happened today and you weren't there. And I'm far away from all the things that used to be normal, and all I can think about is you. And everywhere I go, and everything I look at, reminds me of you. I sit down in a café and I wish you were with me so we could take our time, play a game of Scrabble, watch the world go by. I eat in restaurants and at every other table are couples, smiling at one another, and I am filled with envy. I've been to ancient temples and spent every minute there wishing you were with me, experiencing it all, sharing an adventure. I came away to think about the reasons life is valuable, and the only thing I can think of – the only thing I know to be true – is that life is valuable when you have someone to share it with. I still don't want any of this. I still can't quite make it real in my head. I love you. I want to come home.

Silence.

OK then.

OK then what?

We can meet up when you get back. But don't think anything has changed. It hasn't. You brought this on yourself.

Don't you miss me at all? Do you even know what day it was yesterday?

Of course I do. But I didn't think it was appropriate to send you a message.

Right. Of course. That would have been a ridiculous thing to do, to send the person you're married to a text on their birthday. Their fortieth birthday.

Silence.

OK then, I'm going to be home in just over a week. I'll come home then. We can talk? It's all I want to do, just talk. I think we owe each other that.

I've got to go.

Don't you miss me at all?

Yes. I do miss you.

Then your voice, which had softened, tightened back up again. I could almost hear the process of you shutting me back out.

I've got to go.

I still love you.

I was ecstatic. You'd spoken to me, and you'd agreed that we'd see each other. You'd said you missed me. Things were going to be OK. I could breathe again.

It was the happiest I had felt for a long time. I went out to eat, and for a change I didn't mind sitting alone. I knew that there was a lot of sorting out ahead for us – I'm not stupid – but I could handle it, I could *live*, if you were willing to do it with me.

That night, I slept for six hours, longer than I'd managed for months. In the morning, I took a flight back down the country to the coast, where I'd planned to spend the second part of my trip. From there, I took a boat out to a tiny island, arriving on a wooden pier in the blazing heat with my wheely case, which I had to drag along the beach to my hut. I would be fine here for a few nights, I thought. How could I not be? The island was a tropical paradise, less than a mile long and half that in width. The white beach I had arrived at was lined by fewer than a dozen 'resorts': a smattering of huts and pods, with beach bars fronting their sleeping quarters and at the very end, a restaurant up on stilts for all the honeymooning couples to watch the sunset from. Naturally, I was the only person there alone, but I resolved to make the best of the beautiful setting, and start to make positive plans for the coming months.

I was in suspended animation during those few days. I walked round the island each morning, spending the afternoons lying on the beach, reading, and the evenings on the verandah of my hut or at one of the beach bars, occasionally sharing a drink and some small talk with other holidaymakers. In front of one of the resorts, someone had constructed a wooden swing, suspended over the green-blue sea, big enough for two and hung at such a height that you could swing your legs in the water below it. One morning, early enough that I had the beach to myself, I entertained myself by trying to capture a photo of me swinging on it. I set up my camera on the sand, switching it onto timer, and then sprinted through the shallows to get to the seat before the shutter clicked. I failed, every time, but I found the series of shots of my back, the swing in the distance, hilarious as I scrolled through them. It would have made you smile. I was excited about showing you them, when we did finally get to speak. It would help dispel the tension and the distance between us if I made you laugh. My being an idiot had always amused you.

I was almost sad to leave the island at the end of my stay, but I was ready – more than ready – to get home. I took a selfie, standing in the mirror in my hut on my final morning. I looked tanned, and tired. I was forty. I was going back to my old life, and I didn't know how things were going to work out. But I was glad I was going, and glad too that I'd come away. Maybe I'd been right after all, that getting away would put things in perspective: but not for me, for you. Nothing had ever changed for me – I had always wanted one thing: to have you back. And now you had broken your silence.

The journey home was long: a boat to the mainland, a bus back to Phnom Penh, and then a flight: first to Kuala Lumpur, then on to London. I was hungry, and tired, and feeling weak by the time my cab dropped me off back at the flat. It was so weird to be home. I'd been dreading being back there, but it wasn't as bleak as I'd remembered when I finally got inside. I hadn't taken the sofa or the TV. Or the bed. I really wanted to sleep.

I took my bag upstairs, and returned to the kitchen to go through the post that you'd left piled up on the side. The buzzer went, and I walked to the window to see who it was. A young man, standing beside his pushbike, cap on his head. I didn't know him. I went down the stairs to open the front door, and as I did so he said my name. Yes? I replied.

I'm here to serve you with these papers.

Non-Molestation Order. Under Section 42 of the Family Law Act 1996

Important notice to the Respondent:
You must obey this order. You should read it carefully. If you do
not understand anything in this order you should go to a solicitor,
Legal Advice Centre or Citizens Advice Bureau. You have a right
to apply to the court to change or cancel the order.

If, without reasonable excuse, you do anything which you are
forbidden from doing by this order, you will be committing
a criminal offence and liable on conviction to a term of
imprisonment not exceeding five years or to a fine or both.

Alternatively, if you do not obey this order, you will be guilty of
contempt of court and may be sent to prison.

The Court heard the Application:
without notice. The court had evidence only from the Applicant.
The order was made in the absence of the Respondent. Having
regard to sections 45(1) and (2) of the Family Law Act 1996, the
court decided to make an order without notice because:

[ ] there is a risk of significant harm to the Applicant,
attributable to the conduct of the Respondent if the order is
not made immediately
[ ] it is likely that the Applicant will be deterred or prevented
from pursuing the application if the order is not made
immediately.

Recital:

Upon the parties having agreed that occupation of the family home pending sale shall be as follows:

The Respondent shall only enter or occupy the property between the following hours:

Alternate weekends from Fridays at 9 a.m. to Mondays at 9 a.m., commencing 3 March.

The Respondent shall not enter or occupy the property at any other time.

On 27 February, District Judge Gibson, sitting at the Family Court at Central Family Court, First Avenue House, 42–49 High Holborn, London, WC1V 6NP considered an application for an order and ordered that:

1. The Respondent is forbidden to:
a)   intimidate, harass or pester the Applicant and must not instruct or encourage any other person to do so;
b)   post or publish any material about these proceedings or about the Applicant in print or on Facebook or on any other social media or in any electronic way and must not instruct or encourage any other person to do so;
c)   telephone, text, email or otherwise contact or attempt to contact the Applicant except through her solicitors.

2. This order shalt be effective against the Respondent once the Respondent is made aware of the terms of this order whether by personal service or otherwise.

3. This order shall last until 28 June at 11.59 p.m. unless it is set aside or varied before then by an order of the court.

4. Rule 18.11 Family Procedure Rules 2010
As this order was made without notice, the Respondent has the right (within 7 days beginning with the date on which this order was served on the Respondent) to apply to the court without waiting until the return date to set aside or vary the order. The Respondent must give or ask the Court to give 48 hours' notice of the application to the Applicant's solicitors.

5. Further Hearing
The application(s) for injunction order and occupation order are listed for further consideration including whether the order should continue before a District Judge sitting in the Central Family Court at First Avenue House, 42–49 High Holborn, London, WC1V 6NP on 21 June at 9 a.m. Time estimate: 1 hour.

6. Costs
Costs reserved.

This order is made without notice to the Respondent.

First statement of the Applicant

Background information:

1.   The Respondent and I met six years ago. I moved in with the Respondent fairly quickly, initially because I was in between properties and needed temporary accommodation. Shortly afterwards I sold my property and purchased a property with the proceeds of that sale, in which we both still live. We hold

the property as joint tenants. We were married two years last April, and separated in November last year.

2. Due to the Respondent's abusive behaviour, I ended our relationship in November. In order to keep myself safe while the divorce and financial settlement were being negotiated, I asked the Respondent to alternate occupation of the home. The Respondent agreed to this arrangement.

3. The Respondent has been physically, emotionally and psychologically abusive.

History of abuse:

1. I hereby set out a history of the Respondent's abuse, and patterns of controlling behaviour. Because I have prepared this statement quickly, owing to the immediacy of my need for protection, it is possible that I have omitted or overlooked further examples which evidence the Respondent's abuse. I have tried to cover all of these, but reserve the right to add to this chronology in order to support future court proceedings. I believe the following establishes why I am urgently in need of the protection of a non-molestation order and an occupation order.

2. Although I believe the Respondent has always behaved in ways I now consider to be abusive, and has often shown controlling and damaging behaviours, these have escalated following our marriage, and again following my ending of our relationship. The Respondent has been obstructive, violent and harassing as I have attempted to negotiate a financial settlement pending the finalisation of our divorce and the sale of our family home. They have repeatedly broken the arrangement we have made to share occupation

of our home. I am now too frightened to spend time in the property alone.

3. The Respondent's behaviour is escalating as they have had to relinquish the control they have held over me for many years. I am constantly frightened about what might happen next. I don't feel safe at home, and I am aware that the Respondent knows where I work as well as the addresses of family and friends whom I have been staying with. I feel desperate, and ask that the courts provide me with the protection I need.

4. The Respondent has been used to controlling whom I talk to. They would often show anger when I spent time with family or friends alone, and would check my phone to monitor my communications with others. The Respondent's behaviour caused me to become isolated from my family and friends, as the Respondent would make me feel uncomfortable when I spoke with other people, by making horrible comments or starting an argument.

5. The Respondent's abusive behaviour escalated following our marriage. They would portray me as being incompetent, neurotic or in other ways ridiculous in front of other people, and would put me down about any number of things. I felt I had to agree with the Respondent's opinions and ideas, as well as plans that were made 'on my behalf', or else I would be subject to verbal abuse and physical threats.

6. The Respondent would frequently accuse me of lying, while repeatedly being dishonest themselves, for example staying out late, while accusing me of often being away from home. This form of 'gaslighting' undermined my sense of self and made me feel both deeply unhappy and, at times, physically unwell.

7. On one occasion the Respondent locked me out of our home. I contacted the police as I couldn't access the property, but when the police arrived, the Respondent gave them access immediately. The Respondent told me that the officers had asked if I had mental health problems. The Respondent said that, had they indicated yes, I would have been subject to the interventions of mental health services. I believe they did this to make me feel fearful of losing my job.

8. The Respondent was also physically abusive during our relationship. This would often happen after the Respondent would accuse me of reneging on a plan to do something, e.g. a meal out or a weekend away, when no such plans had been made. On one occasion last autumn the Respondent slammed a door so violently that it caused a picture to fall to the floor and break. The Respondent also punched the wall, and I felt threatened that I would also be punched. There have been many times when I have felt I am in physical danger.

9. During January of last year, the Respondent had become very angry following a night spent in the company of mutual friends. The Respondent felt I had been undermining, which was not the case. Once alone in the flat, the Respondent had become very angry, and had thrown an item of furniture at me, and had prevented me from going upstairs by physically blocking my way. When I took a seat on the sofa the Respondent came over to me and started to push me backwards, their hands on my shoulders. I was very frightened. I didn't retaliate, but the Respondent moved position and squeezed one hand around my neck, which terrified me. I believed I was going to die. After this incident I contacted a domestic violence helpline for support.

10. In the summer of last year, I arrived home to find the Respondent furious because I was late for dinner. I went to the bedroom to avoid a confrontation, but the Respondent followed me and approached where I was sitting on the bed. The Respondent swung an arm out towards me, with clenched fists, but I moved away and they made contact with the wall behind my head instead. I believe it was their intention to punch me in the face.

11. On 14 November I told the Respondent that I wanted to end our relationship. The Respondent became physically very aggressive, calling me vengeful and unbalanced, and putting their hands in my face and pushing me in my chest to stop me from leaving. I was very frightened for my own safety. I believe that the Respondent would take any steps they could to prevent me from seeking a divorce.

12. Following this, I was forced to block the Respondent's number on my mobile phone, because of the number of text messages and phone calls I was bombarded with on a daily basis. I informed the Respondent that I would only be contactable via email, as I felt this was the safest way to communicate, and to maintain some sort of distance between us.

13. Over Christmas and New Year, I went to stay with my sister and her husband. Shortly after arriving there, I heard a knock at the front door, which I answered. I was shocked to see the Respondent standing outside, and became very anxious as I did not know how they would behave, so I attempted to leave the property and walk away. However, the Respondent moved towards the front door and physically blocked my path, repeatedly saying, 'Don't do this, you've ruined my life. Do you want it to end this way?' I asked the

Respondent to move out of my way and let me walk down the path and away from them, but they would not allow me to. I was extremely upset and began to cry and after several minutes, the Respondent eventually stepped aside and I walked down the path away from the front door.

As I attempted to leave the property via the gate at the end of the path, the Respondent followed me and stood in front of me to block my exit. The Respondent was very angry and grabbed the collar of my coat and pulled me towards them, close to my face. I was terrified because the Respondent was so aggressive and intimidating. The Respondent said to me, 'Is this threatening enough for you? Is it?' and still crying, I repeatedly begged to be left alone.

The Respondent eventually let go of me. I believe that now that the Respondent cannot manipulate me through emotional abuse, they are increasingly quick to resort to physical threats in order to force me to agree with them. I was so confused and upset by this incident that I quickly walked away from my sister's home, not knowing where I was going but suddenly the Respondent appeared again and stood in front of me, blocking my way forward. I was a little way down the road from my sister's home, and the Respondent was following me, shouting obscenities at me. Fortunately, there were many people out on the street at the time. I carried on walking and the Respondent eventually stopped following me as there were a lot of people to witness their behaviour. I was so afraid of what the Respondent might do during this incident and I was very shaken.

When I returned to my sister's home, I knocked at the door to be let back in and I was shaking so badly my sister believed I had been assaulted. She told me that I should contact the police but I didn't want to at that time. I believe the incident to be another example of the Respondent attempting to show their power over me, and that they can continue to control me even outside of the setting of our home.

14. The Respondent also continuously telephoned and messaged my sister and my sister's husband to demand to speak to me throughout the Christmas and New Year break. The Respondent threatened to 'do something stupid', so I felt forced to respond. This is another example of the Respondent attempting to control me through their own actions.

15. In January of this year, I arrived back at the family home according to the agreement that had been made to share use of the property. I was deeply alarmed to find the Respondent inside, and went to leave immediately. I was panicking. I reminded the Respondent that they were not meant to be there. They simply laughed at me, before walking down the stairs and forcing their way past me, in order to block my exit from the flat.

The Respondent said they were confused about which day of the week they were due to leave the property, because the Christmas break had disoriented them. I believe this to be completely disingenuous, and further demonstration of the Respondent's capacity to lie to suit their needs.

I was terrified of what the Respondent might do, so I pushed past them and managed to get out onto the street. As I was walking away, the Respondent appeared by my side. I asked the Respondent to leave me alone. They said they would not, and that this time they would force me into a conversation with them. I was very frightened by this.

I was in a state of confusion, and headed to the closest shop, not far from our home. My sole aim was to get away from the Respondent. The Respondent followed me into the shop, and continued to demand that I have a conversation with them. I did not reply. I was panicking. I decided to call my solicitor for instruction as I did not know what to do. My solicitor advised me to report the incident as harassment at my nearest police station.

I followed this instruction, and left the shop and began to walk towards the police station at the top of the Narrow Way in Hackney. Initially, I believed the Respondent had remained in the shop. I was therefore extremely alarmed to find them in front of me as I got to the end of the road. Again, I felt very frightened.

The Respondent was in a rage. They aggressively grabbed me by my jacket and pulled me forward so that our faces were almost touching. The Respondent said, 'I will not put up with this any longer.' I did not know how to react, so stayed absolutely still for a moment, then shook the Respondent's hands off me and backed away from them. As I got a little further away, the Respondent advanced and physically pulled me back by my shoulder, propelling me towards them. The Respondent then aggressively pushed me against a shop front and leaned up against me. I couldn't move away. The Respondent said we must look like lovers. I was terrified that they were going to molest me. Again, I felt sick. I managed to duck underneath the Respondent's arm, and started to run away up the street. I could hear the Respondent shouting behind me. They were accusing me of making up lies with my sister about them in language that I found very upsetting. I heard the Respondent finally shout that I had 'ruined their life', but I was by this time quite a distance away.

This experience was terrifying. The Respondent followed me, physically assaulted me, and verbally abused me. The Respondent is not afraid to act in these ways towards me, as they are accustomed to having me accept such behaviours and even try to cover for them when they have acted in such ways in a public setting.

Following this incident, I went back to my sister's house for the remainder of the day. I didn't return to the family home until the morning after, and I took my sister with me in case the Respondent was still there.

I reported this incident to the police the following Monday, and was told that it was in the police's powers to arrest the Respondent. I decided I did not wish to press charges, I simply wanted the Respondent to leave me alone. The matter was given the incident number 4690568/28. I did not want to cause further unnecessary trouble or to add to the conflict between the Respondent and myself.

I also attended a local domestic violence drop-in centre where I explained the circumstances of my relationship with the Respondent, and was given appropriate support. I remain very frightened that the Respondent will continue to disregard the conditions of our shared use of the family home, and will further continue to threaten me and to enact abusive and violent behaviours.

When I did finally re-enter the family home, I found that the Respondent had removed most of the property from inside. This included almost all the fixtures and fittings, the furniture, and personal items belonging to me. I was deeply distressed by this. Some of the items that have been removed are irreplaceable, and of great sentimental value to me, including gifts from my family members. I believe this action was intended to frighten and upset me, and to create an unbearable living situation for me. I also believe it demonstrates that the Respondent has no sense of what is rightfully theirs.

16. During the Respondent's trip to Cambodia this month, I received a barrage of calls and messages. The Respondent insisted we attend counselling together. I believe that the Respondent was attempting to manipulate me once more and I refused the offer. The Respondent also informed me that they intended to alter the arrangement we currently have in respect of the occupation of the family home. I was terrified by the Respondent's insistence that, on their return home, we would resume shared occupation of the family home, as there was nothing to stop us from doing so.

17. The Respondent's behaviour has escalated once more in the past month. The Respondent will go to great lengths to contact and confront me, despite repeated requests for them to not do so, and even when they are out of the country, in a different continent and time zone.

18. The Respondent cannot comprehend that our relationship is over. I believe that the Respondent represents a threat to me and to those around me. I therefore feel I now need the protection of a non-molestation order and an order regulating occupation of our property.

19. In light of the above, I respectfully ask the court to make a non-molestation order and occupation order in the terms above. I need to know that I am safe in my own home while I negotiate with the Respondent towards a financial settlement that will bring our association to an end. To date, I have

made generous offers to settle our affairs but the Respondent has refused them. I believe the Respondent will drag out proceedings in order to sustain contact with me. I understand that negotiations may take some time, during which I need to keep myself safe.

20. The Respondent can visit the property on alternate weekends, vacating the property while I am there. I am content to be inconvenienced myself, by vacating the property every other weekend. I offer this as a compromise, but I need this arrangement to be enforced by order, as I do not trust the Respondent to stay away from the property when I am there. The Respondent has no reason to return to the property while I am there.

21. For these reasons I ask the honourable court to protect me by granting the orders sought. Such orders are necessary because of the Respondent's history of violence, control and domestic abuse.

22. I respectfully ask that these orders are made urgently, on a without-notice basis. I believe that the Respondent would try to stop me from making the application if they were put on notice of such proceedings. I therefore request the court to make a non-molestation order and occupation order without notice to the Respondent.

March

I had a panic attack when I opened the papers. A full-on, I-can't-breathe, I'm-going-to-die attack, that left me slumped against the wall at the top of the stairs where I'd sat down to read them. It took a long time for me to regain composure, of sorts. I have never felt so scared. I'd never expected to experience the kind of utter, heartless betrayal that you enacted on me that day. I had no way of dealing with it.

I knew I needed help. Things were so out of control. I'd managed so far by calling on a family friend to help draft the few letters I'd had to send to your shitty legal team, rebuffing their demands that I agree to your terms, sending across financial details that would counter your narrative that you were owed everything.

But this was something else.

It all, finally, fell into place. You'd told them a story that meant you could take occupation of the house. You had generously allowed for me to be there every other weekend, a sign of your magnanimity and fortitude, in spite of your need for an order to prevent me 'molesting' you.

I couldn't think of anything less enticing.

You had enlisted your sister to concoct with you a series of lies that described somebody I don't know. You don't know them either. They're not me. They don't exist.

This abuse narrative would then support your claim for a greater share of the proceeds from the sale of the flat. You needed the money to buy a place near our flat, where you had your 'support network'. That network was your manipulative sister. Or perhaps manipulated? Did she even understand that you were making it all up? She wasn't very bright. It was entirely possible you'd deluded her as well.

Did you even know, now, that you were lying? Had it become such a rounded story in your mind that you'd forgotten who I really am? Yes, I believe this now. You have spent a lifetime carefully constructing a version of yourself that you think people will like: you're a master at revising reality to fit that narrative. The abusive dad that you now idolise, retelling his controlling fury as the symptoms of a gentle, misunderstood and generous man so you don't have to face the more prosaic truth that he showed no love to any of the women in his life. The caring listener that you pretend to be, carving out a career that proves your credentials, all the while refusing to really hear when the people around you so desperately need you to listen.

I see now why you work with dying people: there's no feedback loop with the dead, no learning curve. No uncertainties. You do your job well or you do it badly: the result is still the same. It's the perfect fit for someone who can't take on opposing views. It's not counselling. It's not-listening.

I think you believe your own story now. It is a wickedness beyond anything I could imagine if you did not. You've taken what you know of me, my vulnerabilities, and twisted them into a monstrous distortion of the truth. And I will never forgive you.

I had once told you that as a teenager I'd sometimes punched my bedroom wall as a way of releasing some of my anxiety and depression. It was a form of self-harm, I suppose. Some people I knew drew razors along their arms, others got hammered on glue or gas. The effect is the same: a moment's relief, a way of displacing the sadness or isolation or confusion. You had used that knowledge against me, characterising my frustrated lashings-out – directed only at hurting myself – into something far more sinister. You'd found other ways to twist parts of who I am into malevolence and wrong-doing: my attempt to stay connected to you, to understand, to talk. All this, you have portrayed as me harassing you. When I tried to speak to you, because I couldn't understand how you could simply end a marriage without a single backward glance, you described me as deranged, controlling, coercive. Whenever I have demonstrated my desperation and fear, you have used it against me, recasting it as evidence of a monster that isn't real. It is not me that is mad, yet you have used all your skills to twist the narrative your way.

I have to hand it to you: you excel at this.

I spoke to the family friend who had helped me with legal advice so far. I had to disclose what had happened. The shame of it. Admitting that my wife had issued an order for me to keep away from her, and my home, because I was violent and abusive. The more you deny that, the more you sound like a liar. Did you know that? I suspect you did.

We agreed I needed to act, and fast. You knew I didn't have money for lawyers – after all I hadn't been secretly saving for months, as you had – and that you were on the front foot with all of this. Every time I returned to thoughts like this, weighing up just how long you must have planned it, I had to stop and take a breath. I just couldn't get my head around it. I still carried with me those long-established feelings of love for you, and I could not believe what you had done to me.

The friend asked me what I wanted to do. The order had an expiry date, so I could simply let it run its course and stay out of your way. I had no problem with the latter, but I couldn't live with the former. I couldn't let this stand, I almost shouted. It isn't true, none of it. It's intolerable to have these things said about me.

So then we need to write a rebuttal, she said. It will take time. You'll need to gather evidence. You'll need to show that you haven't acted in any of the ways she describes. And then we need to move forward with getting the flat sold as quickly as possible so you can get out of this mess, and move on with your life. I know you haven't wanted to do that up to now. I'm so sorry this is happening to you. But I hope you'll see now that you just need to get things sorted. It's in your own best interests to get as far away from all of this as you can.

I had the flat to myself for the weekend, before I would be court-ordered away. So I spent it at my laptop, going through what you'd said in order to have me excised from your life. I thought back to finding the early version of these stories, that file that had frightened me so much, before I'd pushed it aside, not believing that you'd really repeat those terrible things.

I wondered if you'd managed to shed a tear or two for your lawyers, to embellish your points? It would have helped, no doubt, that you looked so small, so harmless. So harmed. I'd always loved that you were compact, petite. Even that you'd now used against me.

Start at the beginning, said the friend. Go through it point by point, and just state the facts. That's all you need to do.

It wasn't true that you'd moved in with me because you were 'in between properties'. You'd moved in to my flat because we wanted to spend every hour we could together, and it was exciting and romantic and you were able to save the cost and hassle of finding another rental. And I'd said I would be happy to keep us both, paying for everything at my old place while we came up with a new plan.

So gallant. What an idiot.

And then when you sold your old flat, you'd been able to put down the deposit for our place, and you'd said you didn't mind, and I promised to contribute by making it the home of your dreams. You left that bit out.

I am not emotionally abusive and controlling. I see clearly now that you have been. This knowledge makes me feel stupid, and ashamed. I have seen hints of this in you, and I have turned away from it, and now I am paying the price.

I haven't broken any arrangement about the regulation of our home: there wasn't one. You laid down an ultimatum and I stupidly said yes, because back then I thought that if I did what you asked, we'd talk. We'd be able to resolve things. I had no idea you'd set your course, and that if I got in the way you'd do everything you could to annihilate me.

I am not angry with you. I am heartbroken. I am broken in more ways than I could have thought possible. I don't trust my own instincts any more: how could I have got you so wrong? What is wrong with me, to have so fundamentally misjudged you?

I did not control who you talked to, and I did not become angry when you spoke to people you were close to. Who are those people, other than your family? Who have I isolated you from, exactly? I realise now your friendship group is so small. The people you confide in get half-stories, approximations of how you feel or what you're doing. I've heard you do it. And yes, maybe I did get upset when you spoke to your sister sometimes, but only ever on your behalf. You would come off the phone in tears because another arrangement had been broken, another plan unmade. Our other friends have borne witness to you being upset by her in this way, on more than one occasion. And there was that terrible week we went away with her, and the others. God, what a torturous few days that was. Your sister tanked up on gin, singing karaoke and picking fights.

I remembered, then, the full misery of that week. Your sister's monopoly on all conversation that evening when I'd got very drunk. How I often got drunk or high when I was in her company, so I could drown out the nonsense, as she droned on about herself. Hell, if I could have drunk from breakfast time and got away with it, I would have. But that weekend, you did something really mad: I'd dropped a glass and smashed it, stumbling forward towards the coffee table, and you'd acted as if I'd thrown it on purpose. You'd both looked at me like I was a murderer, and you pretended you'd seen me throw it. I was totally baffled, and too drunk to really comprehend what was happening. I didn't know you had it in you to pretend so well. Not then. And in the morning you'd brushed it all away, saying we'd all had too much to drink and I ought to apologise and then we'd all forget about it. What an accomplished performance you'd given. If I'd have been a bit smarter, I should have known then what lay in store for me now.

I remembered, too, the argument we'd had about a stupid photo of your sister that you'd set as your screensaver. You'd showed it to me the day we'd got home from that weekend, taunting me about what a happy couple the two of you made. I knew you were trying to be playful, trying to lighten the mood, but the context was weird, and I made the mistake of saying so. You got upset, saying I was always taking the piss out of you, telling me I was jealous that you had such a loving family. Such a fun family. I said I didn't experience them that way, and you were so upset that I backed down. I hated it when I hurt you, more so when I hadn't meant to. Your sister was always a thorn in my side.

Wasn't it her that claimed I'd stopped you putting family photos up on our walls? I checked back through the copy I'd made of that terrible transcript, the one I'd found under our bed when I'd packed up the flat that mad, frantic few days at the end of last year. I went through it again, line by line, seeing the progression of your story from its roots in that first meeting to where we were now. The plot you'd started to script, in secret, while I thought we were happily married – or at least I thought we were trying to be – and how it had grown and twisted and mutated into the story that I was now at the centre of only a few short weeks later. How quickly poison takes hold.

Yes, I saw that your sister had made the photo accusation. I remembered that I'd gone through the photostream on my phone, scouring it for evidence of what had been mounted on our walls. Counting off the photos we'd printed and hung of your parents, your sister, her kids. Counting, as well, those of my family, so fewer in number. Another lie. Another weirdness, so hard to decipher. Why did she care? Was it her that had said it in the first place? Why did any of it matter?

It was your sister who most often took the piss out of you, portraying you as incompetent. Not me. She made it the subject of her speech at our wedding, making joke after joke about where, when and how you'd lost things. Did she envy you, and what we had built together? Or did you trick me into thinking she was a problem when you were the one playing games? Either way, you'd laughed your head off at her jokes that day. And it was part of who you were; you played on your airheaded tendencies to get people to do things for you. It worked like a charm. And now suddenly, you claimed to be hurt by being made to look ridiculous. But not by me, babe. It wasn't me.

And it wasn't me that wasted police time, calling them out after staying away all night. I think that was the beginning of the end. I was so frightened that night, I didn't know if you were dead or alive. I kept thinking that you couldn't possibly be OK and just not responding, that something terrible must have happened to stop you letting me know where you were. It blows my mind that you just checked in to a hotel somewhere and got a happy eight hours' sleep. What were you thinking? But you got caught out, because you'd gone too far. I'd called your mum, and in doing so, had called your bluff. Suddenly someone else knew what you were up to, which wasn't part of the plan, was it? I was so freaked out when you got back to the flat and started banging on the door. I admit that I'd double locked it as a way of reasserting some pathetic semblance of control. But you carried on so much, banging on the door and shouting, that you hadn't noticed I'd unlocked it ages before you stopped knocking. I wonder if you were scared when you saw the blue lights coming up the street. I was terrified. But not as scared as when you finally came in, shivering and looking brutalised. I thought something must have happened to you. It took a while for me to realise you'd called them because of me. I'd only been able to calm down because the police officer that came into the flat took me to one side and asked if you had any history of mental illness. He thought you were deranged. The terrible thing is, I think he's right. I should have said yes to him, and seen what happened next. But of course I would never betray you like that.

That's your job.

*

I started to realise there were holes in your story, spaces where the inventions were so grotesque, you couldn't possibly produce evidence for them. The tightness round my throat loosened, just a little. All I had to do was write a clear account of what had really transpired. I had to be methodical.

And so, little by little, I drafted a response to the order. I wrote a rebuttal to your story, paragraph by agonising paragraph, retelling the story of my life with you from a perspective not twisted by your dishonesty. It was exhausting. I wracked my brains to think of ways to prove that what I was saying was true. I was terrified I might not be believed, that the order would stand. I knew I would not be able to manage that.

I found all the paperwork from the renovations on the flat. I congratulated myself on my OCD-like filing, taking delight in the thick catalogue I'd created with receipts and invoices. They told the story of my year as a builder, chronicling every trip to buy materials or order fixtures and fittings. They vindicated me: you'd put down the deposit on the flat, and I'd matched you with a year of my life, putting my body down in every room, on every improvement I'd made. And I had the receipts to show what I'd paid for, how much I'd invested. I couldn't prove the toll it had taken on my body, but I could show that my finances had taken hit after hit.

It was a start. A way of tilting the story towards the truth. But it wasn't enough, I knew that. The order hadn't been granted because the judge thought I'd stinted on my contribution to our bank account. It had been granted because he thought you were scared, and in danger. And it wasn't as easy to prove you had lied about that.

All I could do was write down my version, and trust that it would be enough to sow seeds of doubt about what you said had happened. I sat for two days at my screen, sifting emails, filing attachments, constructing my defence. You will never know how disgusted I was by this process. Part of me was so outraged that I didn't want to dignify your lies with a response. But it had been made clear to me, in no uncertain terms, that taking the moral high ground was no longer an option.

I could see how easily you'd twisted little things into big, ugly events. Yes, I'd slammed the door of our bedroom during one of our rows. And yes, a picture had fallen to the floor. But not because of me. You missed out the bit where you'd followed up my slam with an almighty, full-body swinging of the door that rocked the walls of the room, and brought the picture that Corinne, my most recent ex, had made for me smashing down onto the floor. If I hadn't been so upset by that, I would probably have laughed. It had been almost comedic, the way you'd thrown yourself with everything you had into making the door crash shut. It wasn't funny now, though. Not now that you'd plugged that gap in your telling of this story with a big fat lie: that I'd punched the wall, and threatened to punch you.

It was mind-blowing, every time I read it. I started to pick out the lines that were real sucker punches, holding them up to the light, congratulating you on your art. Yep, that was a really good one. I had to hand it to you. I considered, for a long time, what you'd said. What it would have looked like, how it would have been for you to feel so threatened. I played it over and over in my head. Where I would have stood. What your face would have looked like. And as I did so, a different image swam to the surface, slowly crystallising behind my eyes, puzzling at first before, eventually, hardening into a picture in my mind's eye that stopped me still.

I don't know why I hadn't remembered it until then. And even when I did, it still seemed unworthy of mention, in spite of everything that was going on. That you had hit me once, full in the face. That there had been punches thrown, yes. But not by me.

Does it count if you're not frightened when you're struck? If you experience someone's fist in your face with disbelief rather than fear? Does that constitute violence? Does it count if you sympathise with the person hitting you, knowing your own capacity for a rigidity that drives them crazy? Does it matter that you've driven someone to the limits of their patience? If you don't blame them, not one bit, when they finally lash out?

And is it violence, really, if you're bigger and stronger than the person hitting you? If it genuinely doesn't hurt? If you experience it only as surprising, and embarrassing, and sad? Does it count if you don't really count it at all?

There was only one person that ever raised their fists to the other during our marriage. It wasn't me. I remembered this not suddenly, but with a slow, dawning consciousness that crept across me, like long shadows at the end of a summer's day, chilling the ground. It hadn't been me. It hadn't, ever, been me.

I sat still for a long time, replaying that fight. Your habit of coming at me, talking over me, grabbing at every single thing I'd ever done wrong and hurling it at me, all at once, in a deluge of accusations that left me unable to come up for air. It felt like grasping at smoke, trying to grab hold of the point I'd been trying to make before it was blown away by your approach. I'd never come out of a single argument with you feeling like I'd made myself clear. I'd never had an apology, even when it seemed so obvious to me that you'd been in the wrong. It was always me that ended up saying sorry, somehow. It was all so fucked up. How had it carried on like that for so long?

I had tried to explain, once, how unmanageable our fights were. I'd been drinking with Nancy, and I'd let slip that I'd slept in the spare room, again. And then I told her about you throwing a knife at me that Christmas, carefully keeping a smile on my face as I recounted the scene. Checking her reaction, clocking her disbelief. She'd been shocked that we'd even gone to bed on an argument, so I didn't reveal how often that had started to happen. I was ashamed. I was ashamed, too, that I couldn't fix the problem of our failed communication. Me, of all people, who prided myself on my articulacy. On crafting a good argument. It all fell apart in the face of your unboundaried attacks.

And then I remembered something else. I had jokingly disclosed the details of that night you'd hit me to another friend. A friend who worked in a counselling service. A friend who didn't think it was at all funny. Which meant that although I had been glib about what had happened – I don't even remember how it came up now – I had had to recant, to say it was nothing, to fluff the ending. I remembered the look on his face. How I'd stopped laughing, and said solemnly that it hadn't been right, it wasn't like that, it was just a silly fight that went wrong. And then I remembered that he'd emailed me the following week, a message that had made me cringe. How I could come to him at any time if I needed to talk. How it was good to seek support. How he was worried about my safety. It was humiliating. I'd mentioned it to you at the time, an awkward confession of what had transpired. You'd met it with silence. I'd left well enough alone.

I had the email. I must still have the email. I returned to my in-box, scouring again to find this crucial piece of evidence. What if it wasn't there? Had I deleted it to avoid this reminder of such a shameful part of our story? I found it, eventually, and felt a brief but still delicious moment of triumph. It didn't disprove what you'd said about me, but it surely cast doubt on your honesty, if nothing else. That was enough for now. I let out just a tiny sigh of relief.

It was a bleak forty-eight hours. I took the occasional rest to sleep, fitfully, or to head out to the shop for packet sandwiches and junk food. I had to hand the house back over to you by Monday morning, and I needed to finish this epic rewrite of our lives by the time I let you back in here. I couldn't make it through the week at work with-out having it set down in words. I needed it set out for my own sanity too, I realised. The more I reread the court order, the less certain I was of my own version of events. I had to get my side down on paper, in black and white, before I lost sight of it completely.

The stories of physical violence were the hardest to face up to. They were both so detailed and sufficiently vague as to make me question, over and over, if they had actually happened. You said that I would block you from leaving a room, which was true, only not in the way you said it. I would stand between you and the door, pleading. But I would never physically move or restrain you. Would I? If I couldn't remember ever doing this, what would cause you to make it up?

Every time I got to this point – the point where I'd sit, puzzled, certain that some memory would surface to explain the confusion – I would remember, with a jolt, that it was a lie. You'd simply made it up. I hadn't pinned you down, or threatened to punch you, or held you hostage. It was almost worse, this realisation, than if your accusation had been true and I had simply forgotten it. I didn't want to believe that you were capable of such malice. How could I have fallen in love with someone so dishonest, so calculating and callous? But page by page, line by line, the court order you'd had served on me tore apart the you I had known. I really didn't like the person left in her place.

There was one story I kept coming back to. It gnawed away at me. I read it over and over, feeling sick and frightened and furiously affronted. Not able, at first, to even set down my refutation of it. Again, some of the details were true and it was this – the inclusion of some part of what I knew was real – that undid me. It was true we had had a terrible argument that night in December. We had scuffled, on the sofa, just like you said. But it was you that had pushed me backwards, shoving me hard to emphasise a point you were making. I had raised my hands, palms towards you, to stop you from doing it again. You had come at me anyway, and my hands had stayed where they were, meeting the top of your chest and blocking you from getting nearer to me. I can remember the moment clearly. I was absolutely still, while you pushed your body against my still-upheld palms. I never moved. You had your eyes on mine the whole time. It was dirty, rotten and sordid. But it wasn't what you had said it was. Nothing like it.

Whichever way you played this scene, it was grubby. In your version, I'd raised my hands to grip around your neck, and squeezed, until you were afraid you'd die.

Pretty grim, even by your standards.

In mine, I'd kept perfectly still until you'd pushed me further away, and I went upstairs to bed, alone. In despair. And just a little more depleted, a little less wholly me, than the day before.

The more I played this scene – over and over in my head – the more I could picture your version of events. I saw myself raise my hand to your neck, saw your body lift slightly upwards as I tightened my grip around you, locking my elbow out as my arm straightened in front of me. I saw the look of panic cross over your face, felt a surge of pleasure as you choked just a little, a sound catching in your throat as you made the effort to breathe. I knew I was being mad, and of course I was horrified by my imagining, but a part of me – a silent, private, beaten part of me – also delighted in it.

In time, this image became almost as vivid as my memory of what had really happened. I guessed this must be what had happened with you, too. That you'd thought it at first, then imagined it over and over, and then made it real by writing it down. By telling it to someone else. What a pity, for me, that you'd told it to a lawyer. And that the lawyer had told it to a judge. And that the judge had believed you.

I think it actually helped, that you'd told a lie that big and foul. It drove me. I returned again and again to the judge's order that weekend, writing and rewriting my account of what had really transpired. Whenever I wavered, and thought of you, and wanted – still – to call you, to attempt a conversation, I conjured up the image of you dangling underneath my grip, and I could continue.

Thank you for that.

And by returning to your chronology of the abuse you accused me of, I began to also see how dishonest and manipulative you were. Through and through. I marvelled at how I'd missed it for all those years. Whenever I'd felt unease at something you'd done, I'd always made it make sense so that my image of you wasn't altered. I was stupidly in love. Very stupidly.

Now, I was able to recall where some of the lies had sprung

from. You said that I'd pushed you up against a wall and threatened you, and as I reread this over that awful weekend, I recalled
you'd told this lie before. It came back to me clearly. We'd been
out walking somewhere, and we were disagreeing about something
we'd been discussing, and I'd spun you round, playfully, by the
waist and lost my balance a bit. I stumbled into you and then immediately righted myself. But you'd said I was hurting you, that
I'd shoved you against a fence on purpose. That I couldn't win
an argument by lashing out. I'd been so shocked that you'd said
it like that, I hadn't even protested. It was such a weird interpre-
tation of reality, I'd thought you must be joking, but I said sorry
anyway and filed it away somewhere inaccessible, in that part of
my brain where the bits of you that didn't make sense stayed safely
away from everything else. Not troubling the delicate equilibrium
I'd constructed so that we worked.

I remember you long ago at a party, whispering behind the backs
of two couples who'd been the best of friends for years. Not just
friends, you'd hissed to one of our most gossipy acquaintances: two
of them have been sleeping together behind the other two's backs.
Didn't you know?

You'd been so convincing, and anyway had known them all for
so much longer than me, that I never questioned that you were telling the truth. I even found it a little bit funny, this sordid insight
into their secret goings-on. But the gossip had got out, of course it
had, and the subject of your lie had been so hurt that she had taken
aside our loose-lipped friend in tears the next time we'd partied together. She couldn't understand why such a lie had been spread. I
was shocked. I asked you why you'd said that of them. And you told
me you hadn't, you'd only heard it yourself that night; you were as
confused as I was.

I knew that didn't make sense, but I felt muddled. I hated to think
that you'd make something like that up, so I buried the memory. And
now here it was, resurrected. A macabre visitor, come back to haunt
me. Evidence of your capacity to tell stories with unhappy endings.

I think you felt an odd power in delivering these versions of other people's lives. I think you enjoyed diminishing them through your slanted portrayals. I think all this now, but I understand none of it.

The court order said I'd lashed out at you over a burned dinner, when in fact you'd come in late, hurled a pile of accusations my way, and then manufactured a reason to storm upstairs and get into bed without an explanation or excuse. I'd pursued you upstairs, yes. And perhaps my fists were closed as I stood limply in the door of our bedroom, looking in at you through tears of frustration.

Because I'd spent all day prepping and cooking that dinner – a wedding anniversary celebration – and you'd simply not turned up. No call, no text, no contact. And then when you'd finally arrived home and seen what state I was in, you'd somehow managed to contrive things so I was the unreasonable one. So when you'd marched upstairs and got into bed, I'd pulled the duvet away from you, in order that I could see your face. I didn't swing a punch at the wall or at you. I swung some high-quality John Lewis duck down off our bed, and then walked out of the room. I had just wanted to talk to you. It was always me, trying to talk to you. It was always you, refusing.

I had overlooked, for a long time, how isolated I had become inside the couple that was us. I didn't disclose any of the chaos. I didn't even think that it was chaotic, after a while. I just got used to feeling alone in your company.

Last May, we went to a big birthday bash at a place on the Kent coast. It was the worst possible time for me, I was so snowed under with work. I had a huge deadline to meet the day that we drove down there, and the day after the party I was due at another event in Spain, which I hadn't even begun to prep for. I'd scheduled in the time I'd have on the flight to write the outline of what I was going to say. I was pretty full up. I was panicking.

I just wanted you to help me, a little. Instead, you were an arsehole. You knew how much work I'd had on, and how little time I'd had to think about the party. I had to make a speech, and sort out some of the live music, and I'd stupidly volunteered to sort out decorating the venue too. I felt totally overwhelmed, which I knew was stupid – it was only a party. But the bookending of the weekend with so much work meant I was feeling beyond stressed. I needed a hug, and some calming words. I needed you.

You'd started being a bit weird in the car, which I'd half-expected. You got edgy on weekends like this, feeling outside of an inner circle that I didn't even notice was there. I hadn't been too worried at first – I was used to it – so when we got to the pub on the beach I'd started to unwind, enjoying the soothing balm of a first cold beer. I was excited about the party, and I was glad to be with friends I hadn't seen for a while. I always loved the build-up to a big night. I loved it that we all made such an effort to have a good time.

As I stood up to leave the pub, I saw you weren't going to come with me. I knew then that you were going to make it a difficult night. You plastered on that fake 'you don't mind' smile, making it impossible for me to say that I did. I really did. I was desperate to get back to our apartment and have some down time, with you, before I had to spend the rest of the afternoon and evening doing the set-up and helping things go smoothly.

I knew you'd make me feel needy if I said I wanted you to come. And you did. But you also got up, eventually, making it abundantly clear to me and everyone else that you'd rather stay where you were. I bit my tongue, keeping the peace, glad that you were coming anyway. I thought it would be OK once we got back to the rental. I thought you could help me write my speech for the birthday boy. I thought we could have some time alone. I even thought we might have sex. I really was a fucking idiot.

Instead, we got back, had a massive row, and I wrote the speech on my own, listening to you getting pissed in the garden below. Then I heard you leave the rental. Then I sat alone, bewildered, hurt and silent. Familiar feelings, all of them. After that, I went to the party venue and got on with my tasks. I noticed a missed call from you, and felt a surge of relief that you were reaching out. But you didn't answer when I called back. It was yet another night where I'd have to act the role of your partner. Not actually be it.

And then later on, when you saw me starting to relax, you told me you wanted me to skip the after-party and head back with you. I'd hardly got going. I'd spent most of the party in organising mode, and just at the point when I'd started to have a good time, you wanted me to call it a night. It was so typically you. And I was so typically me, refusing to come to heel and staying out all night instead, judging it best to sleep on a friend's floor than come in at a stupid hour and wake you. What were we doing? Wasn't it so clear that we just didn't fit together? Why did it have to come to this?

Control. That's what it was all about, in the end. Your model for a marriage, learned from your dad, was of one person controlling the other. You were smart enough not to adopt the role of submissive wife – although you were playing a blinder in pretending – but not clever enough to perceive that you'd inherited these destructive patterns of behaviour from your parents. That's what I began to conclude, anyway, as I wrote my painful rebuttal to your claims of abuse. If only you'd been to therapy, baby, instead of foisting couples counselling onto both of us. You can't fix a crumbling house if the bricks you try to rebuild it with are shot through.

You'd reverted to type, then, when things started going wrong. Take control, ignore the pain you inflict, look after number one. Since you couldn't control me after all, you took over the narrative of our lives, rewriting it so you came out of our marriage with enough money, enough sympathy, enough of a reason to leave in the way you did. I figured all this out as I untangled the stories you'd told, noting how you must have roped your sister in since she featured so many times in the telling of this alternative reality. Unless… was it really possible that you'd duped her along with everyone else?

I wrote down what had happened that day I'd dropped a Christmas present at her door – which you'd slammed in my face. It was true that you'd then come outside. You must have thought I'd left, but I was standing against a tree at the end of your sister's path, willing my traitorous legs to solidify, to carry me away. They'd given way with the sight of you.

I can still remember, with absolute clarity, my heart jumping when I thought, just for a second, you'd come out to talk to me. And then it freefalling when I saw the thunderous look on your face, and realised how stupidly wrong I was. It wasn't true that I'd then grabbed you and pulled you about.

How could I ever have done that?

I was holding on to the idea that something remained, and I tried to tell you that. I tried to tell you the power you had over me. I was still pretending, to myself, that I held the same over you. I appealed to two passers-by to tell you that, explaining that you were my wife. My life. Asking them to intervene on my behalf. A stupid, romantic, pointless gesture. And then I left, taking your silence as agreement that maybe something remained, holding onto that tiny bit of hope.

It had faded very quickly, and so I'd spent the Christmas break desperately trying to talk to you, to rekindle that sputtering spark of optimism. I am embarrassed, now, to recall the messages I left. For you, for your sister, for your mum, pleading for you to get in touch. Hiding in my old bedroom at my parents' house, calling the numbers over and over again. It is no wonder my mum insisted I go to the doctor's when I got home, nagging at me until the appointment was made, then listening quietly as I told her what had been prescribed. Beta blockers for the panic, sleeping pills for the insomnia, a psych assessment just a few days later. I dug out the paperwork that had been generated from this – evidence, for my rebuttal, of the damage you'd done to me. It noted that although I had started to feel a little better by the time I spoke to the psychologist in mid-January, I still struggled with thoughts that life was not worth living. I hadn't told them that I just couldn't figure out a way to end it.

Over that long weekend of writing, I wrestled down my version of events. It was easy when I could start a sentence with 'I have never', which I did, a lot, but your clever trick of including some details that were true made my account more tentative, more complicated. I hoped it didn't make it less convincing. The 'furniture' I'd once thrown towards you was a cushion, I wrote, tossed in the air in frustration, an attempt to distract you from your criticism of me on the night you claimed I'd tried to strangle you. Had you really contacted a DV helpline that night? Had you decided, even then, that this was the way you were going to go?

And then, again, you said you'd attended a domestic violence drop-in centre, earlier this year, after that terrible morning when I'd seen you at the flat. Had you? How dare you if you had. How dare you use their services to further your campaign for a tidy divorce payout, and for a rock-solid backstory to your bailing on our marriage. It sickened me. I wanted to tell everyone who knew us what you'd done. But of course that would reveal what you were alleging. And once that seed has been sown it always leaves a tiny shoot of doubt.

You must have known that. You were a better strategist than I'd ever considered.

I took pleasure in pouring scorn on your version of our last meeting, that awful morning in January when you said you'd gone to the police. It shook me to see that written down. And then, unexpectedly, I shook with laughter at the idea you'd resisted pressing charges to avoid causing me 'unnecessary trouble'. Ha!

I think that was my favourite line, in the end.

Finally, I got to the last element of your story. Your closing scene. The recasting of that conversation I'd had with you as I sat by a pool in Cambodia – the first for months – as an attempt by me to threaten you. As a manipulation. It was hard to believe, by the time I wrote my version out on that Sunday, that only forty-eight hours earlier I'd arrived home with my happy secret: I was going to see you. You'd agreed to us meeting, a knowledge I'd kept close to my chest all the way home, a tiny item of additional luggage collected during my time away. I had to admit, it was humiliating I'd got you so wrong.

It hadn't occurred to me, not once during that long journey home, that you'd rescind on the plan, that you'd use it against me. I felt that now-familiar jab of disgust as I imagined you telling your version of our conversation to your lawyer. Omitting the part where you told me you missed me; modifying my suggestion that we meet at home, together, to arrange our separation more kindly.

So I detailed the alternative version of our little chat, remembering the feeling of cool blue water lapping over my feet as we talked. Sitting poolside, the day after I'd turned forty, believing that better things were finally just around the corner. I really should have known by then. I really should have guessed.

I signed off my rebuttal with a flourish: I have never been violent. I am not abusive. I am not angry and I have never been controlling. There is nothing to evidence these claims, as they are simply untrue. I find it hard to believe that my wife does not wish to cause me unnecessary trouble, given the inaccuracies in her account. She has made a derisory offer for a financial settlement and subsequently refused to consider any counter-offer. I am clear that my relationship with her is over.

I was pleased with my final lines: 'I was understandably devastated by the manner in which the Applicant ended our marriage, and have found it difficult to understand her callousness in refusing all contact, including mediation. It is my belief now that she has created and sustained a false and incriminating narrative about me and about our lives together, in order to benefit from our divorce. The court orders she has sought to put in place are part of her strategy for finalising proceedings between us both quickly and, for her, advantageously.'

Fuck you, wife. Fuck you.

I left the flat on Monday, and returned to work. It was strange to be back in my normal life, where nothing was normal any more. I found it hard to slot myself back into the hole I'd left behind when I set off for Asia. I didn't fit any more. I was changing shape, filling out, becoming a bigger version of the me that had cowered and cried for the past four months. It was about time.

I went to the Central Family Court to file my rebuttal, and the bits of paperwork I'd scrabbled together as supporting evidence. I was guided through security, emptying my pockets, placing my bag on the conveyer belt. Both it and I were scanned, inspected. Then I took my place in a queue with the wife-beaters and abused women that were there that day, seeking vengeance or protection. Rage and fear seeping out of the walls of a grimy, stained-ceilinged collection of corridors and rooms. Another new low. I deposited my file, took my receipt and left as quickly as I could, not wanting to be associated with these lives, this despair. I had applied for the order to be set aside. Now I just had to wait.

I took the advice I'd been offered, and made an appointment with a barrister. Erica Jong. I got a real kick out of that. The namesake of a feminist icon was to represent me: it seemed like a good omen. I needed some equal opportunity; I'd been on the back foot for so long. I met with her at her chambers, a few rooms in one of the smart townhouses on Bedford Row.

First things first, she said. Have you submitted your rebuttal to the non-molestation and occupation order? I looked down at the floor. But what point was there now in feeling humiliation? I was here to put my cards on the table, to front up to what had been done. Done to me, not by me. I had nothing to hide, but it was hard not to feel guilty. You'd done a tremendous job of labelling me a monster. I half believed it myself now.

Yes, it's all done, I said. I met her eye. She smiled at me, warmly. Then she set it all out. Our gameplay for the next few weeks.

You've applied for a court date so that your side of things can be heard. This may or may not be scheduled before the date that the orders are due to be reviewed: because they were granted as an emergency, they expire in a few weeks as the judge will expect to hear what your response will be. Based on what you told me over the phone, and the evidence you were able to produce, the orders will not be upheld. Your application to have them set aside will have been sent to your wife's solicitors, and so I would expect that you will hear from them shortly. It may be that they let you take this back to court, but I would expect that they will offer to settle this with cross-undertakings: that is, you both have to promise the court that you will not do again that which you deny ever having done!

I laughed, just a little. It felt really good to have this woman on my side. I could tell she believed me. I was profoundly grateful.

She continued. Usually, in injunction proceedings the issues boil down to six of one and half a dozen of the other. However, from what I have read, your wife has manufactured a statement based on a set of events that didn't take place. There is a case to be made that issuing spurious proceedings is tantamount to harassment, an attempt to intimidate you as you're engaged in negotiating a financial settlement.

My heart jumped. She had just said what I knew to be true, and I felt momentarily exhilarated at the idea of turning the tables. Of going after you just as you had me. Justice.

And revenge, I had to admit.

However, as you now know, your wife 'presents' well as a victim. I realise it's an awful thing to say. But judges respond to it. Your wife's legal team will have used it to their advantage. She would have been in court in person, you know, to get these orders issued?

I didn't know that. Immediately, though, I could picture it. You standing tiny in a dock, looking pleadingly to the judge for help. I embellished my own mental image, positioning an avuncular, kindly man in the judge's chair, looking pityingly on this tremulous, cowed woman in his courtroom, silently weeping. The more grotesque the picture became, the more I was able to disengage from the you that I'd known.

It was good to focus on this other person.

So I suggest we start with asking that the orders be discharged, and see what they come back with, said Erica. There will need to be an edict of some sort that sets out when you can both use the flat, so think about what you want and we can go from there.

I nodded. I wouldn't ask for anything more than I already had, as I dreaded being at home. Home wasn't really a word that made sense any more, in this context. Checking in at the flat every other weekend was about as much as I could bear. And anyway Zed was about to head overseas for three months, so had offered me a temporary alternative, which I'd gladly accepted.

I just want to leave things as they are, I said. Minus the court order.

That's fine. We'll write a 'without prejudice' letter making it clear that you have not harassed their client nor have you intimidated or threatened her. We'll also state that you have suffered harassment, intimidation and threats from her. We'll say you are reluctantly prepared to settle the matter on the basis of cross-undertakings and we'll set out terms for occupying the flat, explaining that you are offering to continue a very generous arrangement by which their client benefits far more than you. And then we'll focus on getting things ready for agreeing a financial settlement. If they won't consider anything you put forward through letters, I'm afraid we're going back to court. But don't worry: next time, I'm coming with you.

I smiled at her. I breathed out. This was worth every penny.

The next day, I received an email from your lawyers. 'We have received copies of the papers you have filed in regard to an order made against you. We understand that you are concerned about these orders and, having consulted our client, she has confirmed she would be willing to accept an undertaking to the court in order to bring the matter to a close. Our client will discharge the existing order if you are prepared to replace it with an undertaking. She is keen to avoid a hearing which might be distressing for both of you.'

I rang Erica. She laughed. She hadn't even written the letter that we'd planned the day before. She congratulated me, explaining that this part, at least, was over. She also said we wouldn't be settling for me making an undertaking to the court: we would demand you also made one, so you would now also be bound by a legal promise. See how you like that. Breaching it would be contempt of court, she explained. It was time to get on the front foot.

You know, she said, this is very good news. Your wife's legal team have recognised the flimsiness of her story. You should feel reassured by that.

I thought about it. I thought, again, about what had really happened on the night you'd accused me of trying to strangle you. Even though I was the only person on earth who could know, for certain, that your story wasn't true, I had been convinced, just a little, by your telling of events.

How mad. You are a really good liar. I had to be very, very careful from now on.

At the end of the week I moved my belongings – a holdall and a bag of snacks – into Zed's place, resolving not to spend any more time in the flat other than the occasional check-in on the weekends it was 'mine'. By then other than my weekends in our flat, I had spent almost three months sleeping in the spare room of our friends' place, and I was pretty sure I was reaching the point where my welcome was outstayed. It was a pull, to give up this bolthole that was so close to our home, my former life. I'd often detoured past the flat on my way to or from work, pathetically hoping to catch a glimpse of you through the window. Experiencing physical pain when I actually did. I knew I couldn't do that any more – I was terrified, still, of being hauled before the courts with further accusations of abuse – but it was another loss. Another snipping of the threads that had bound us to one another. I had to start seeing that severance as a good thing: a disentanglement of something dysfunctional, and destructive.

It was a hard adjustment to make.

Things helped. Like the night I had a phone call from an old friend, who'd been out with you several weeks back, meeting you for a drink some time after Christmas. She told me that you'd sought her out, and she'd been surprised that you wanted to meet up. You'd never been that close but she was glad that you'd reached out. And so you'd gone to the pub and done all the usual chat and then she'd asked you about things with me and you'd begun telling your story to her. Not all of it – the details had obviously come later, when you wanted to accelerate the process of getting rid of me. But you'd practised the routine on her, lowering your voice, beginning to cry, explaining how controlling I was and how frightened you'd been to leave.

'It didn't sound like it could be you she was describing.'

It wasn't. It was a new version of me that had been recently invented. One that sounds like a psychopath, but that only exists in your head.

I took on this new information, vacillating between revulsion and rage.

Did you believe her? I asked over and over again.

Well, she was so convincing. It felt wrong, what she was saying, but I didn't feel I could question her. Do you know how difficult it is to question someone's experience of something like that? I had to believe what she was saying was true. I'm so sorry.

My friend started to cry. I comforted her, said it didn't matter now. And it didn't. It felt good to talk about it, to bring into the light this shameful secret that I'd been hiding. I hadn't wanted to expose it – me – to scrutiny. I was too frightened I wouldn't stand up to it.

But I could. I did.

I was believed, and in that moment, it was enough.

It hasn't left me, that burning sense of the injustice of your lies. I use it, still, to harden my heart against you in the moments when I wonder where you are now, and how you're doing. When I want to hear your voice. When I wake in the night having dreamed that we met again, and you said sorry, and you held me. I summon the image of me holding you by the throat, and I remember why this picture exists. And then I squeeze, just a little harder.

After all, it's just a story.

Hendry, Price LLP, Family Law Practice, 13 March: transcript of consultation regarding financial settlement and court action. With Michelle Hendry, solicitor.

To be delivered by hand.

The purpose of today's meeting was to review our work with you to date, and to prepare for next steps regarding your financial settlement.

You were concerned that J still has access to the family home, but it was explained that concluding the actions taken against J were in everyone's best interests.

You are keen to move to a situation where you can negotiate a sensible financial settlement. We discussed our concern that allegations and counter-allegations would serve little purpose and would further destroy any goodwill between you and J. I explained that I would write to J to communicate this, and to seek assurance that this cooperative approach would be reciprocated.

To date, we have made a 'without prejudice' offer to J which you considered extremely generous. This would amount to a 75 per cent/25 per cent split of the proceeds of sale from the family home in your favour. You were very disappointed that J was not open to this offer, and dispute J's claims about contributing to the building work that saw the property transformed into its current condition. J has argued that it is by dint of their physical labour over a period of more than a year, as well as investment in materials and tools, that the property's value doubled during the time you shared residence in it. You have countered that both of you undertook redecoration, as most couples do, although you acknowledge you cannot evidence your input in any detail.

You further counter that the increase in equity is due to property inflation rather than J's hard work and endeavour. However, J has provided an estate agent's valuation of the flat made immediately after completion of the renovation works, which show a gain in the value of the property of more than 50 per cent in your first year of ownership.

J has further written to us to set out the disparity between your separate accounts of your shared finances. J alleges that you acquired the deposit for the purchase of the family home through the sale of a housing association property, the tenancy for which you had assumed by deception. This is immaterial to the matters of this case, but you were worried it might be something J would refer to should your matter proceed to court.

J also alleges that you came to a mutual agreement, on the occasion of your deciding to buy a home together, that your contribution would be the deposit while J would contribute through the suspension of their career for 18 months and the undertaking of the renovations. J states that the planning and renovations, including identifying the property and carrying out the works, was solely their endeavour; and as stated above, that it is only through such endeavour that the family home has attained its current value. Following the completion of the works, J returned to full-time work. J has indicated that you remain employed on only a part-time basis, and could therefore increase your earning capacity by taking on more hours at work. You were very clear that this was not an option: you work in a highly pressurised environment which is enormously emotionally and psychologically draining.

We have noted J's response to the wording of our initial offer, which referred to your two-year marriage: J emphasised that this is not simply a 'two-year marriage' but a marriage that followed seamlessly from a four-year cohabitation and that the family home was purchased during the cohabitation and prior to the marriage.

You are clear that you put the deposit down on the property – a fact that J does not dispute – and met all the mortgage repayments during the period of your relationship with J. In response, J has claimed that while you paid the mortgage, they paid an equivalent amount into a joint account from which all bills and living expenses were met, making the arrangement equitable. There is evidence of this from J's Form E.

J has also contested the amount that you deposited in order to secure the purchase of the flat, as well as the amount you contributed to renovations. You accept that you were wrong in your early calculations of these sums, your mistakes arising from the extreme stress you were under at the time you first informed J of your intention to end your marriage.

Following our initial offer, we received a counter-offer from J which put forward a different division of the proceeds from the sale of the family home, also split in your favour. J stated that the proposals we had put forward would not allow them to rehouse in suitable accommodation, and that our suggestion that they relocate to south London was unacceptable. J further argued that their counter-offer was generous, since the starting point for the division of assets in any marriage is 50/50.

J stated that they were willing to offer you a more-than-equal split in order to expedite proceedings and obviate the need for any future wrangling, which would be highly distressing. J also noted your refusal to attend mediation in order to discuss a settlement face to face.

We feel it is unfortunate that it has not been possible to negotiate a financial settlement directly. We understand that this is what you had hoped for, but the details of your case have not proven to be as straightforward as we'd first imagined.

You asked me to set out a worst-case scenario for you: in your case, I would expect that the worst-case scenario would be a 50/50 division, since that is what the law is based on, but that we would hope to argue in court for nearer 70/30, based on what you have told us about your and J's contributions. Of course, we will only succeed in this if the evidence you submit is accurate and verifiable.

We note that J has been very efficient in providing the financial information we have requested in order to move forward on a settlement. We advised you that the process now is to move forwards towards an initial First Directions Appointment. Ahead of this we will have to file a number of forms with the court, along with a summary of the issues. If all the required information is provided it is possible to treat this hearing as an 'FDR', a Financial Dispute Resolution. I explained that this is a 'without prejudice' hearing, which gives us the opportunity to negotiate a final financial settlement with the input and assistance of a family judge. We will prepare arguments and present them in a courtroom, and J must do the same. It is possible that, if we are able to agree a settlement with J's legal team on the day of the FDR, we will draft a final order that will be signed off by the judge. That will bring your matter to an end. If we don't reach a settlement, the judge will list the case for a trial.

We will emphasise your desire to work towards a less acrimonious approach with a view to final settlement.

You asked that we make a final offer of settlement ahead of moving forward with an FDA. We agreed to your request that we offer a significantly lower amount than your first 'without prejudice' offer, bearing in mind the uncertainty of future arrangements and J's current precarious living situation, all of which you feel might serve to focus J's mind and make a quick settlement a more attractive prospect.

We will outline the contribution you made in paying the deposit and associated legal fees when you bought the flat, as well as your payment of the mortgage in its entirety to date. We will offer to deduct this amount from the proceeds of sale and return it to you, and then split the remaining proceeds 60/40 in your favour. This will leave J with less than 25 per cent of the total proceeds of sale. We will reserve the right to refer the court to this offer, made in good faith, if it is declined and matters proceed to a hearing. This will be beneficial to our case in relation to the issue of costs, showing that we have attempted to avoid the need to bring this matter before the court.

Court action is enormously stressful and will be costly for both of you; J will have to engage a legal team, making the process more combative – to date, J has self-represented throughout all correspondences with our offices and has claimed to have had no legal representation, although you believe that some form of informal support is in place.

You said you had borrowed money from your mother in order to cover your legal costs so far. We will show that you have not only made considerable investment in your legal services but have also covered the expense of having to spend every other weekend away from the family home in order to allow J access. I reassured you that we would include consideration of these costs in our negotiation of the final settlement.

You hope that in spite of the disagreements between you and J, you will both be able to agree that escalating legal costs are in neither of your best interests. We have discussed the reasons for your declining mediation, and you are adamant that you wish to proceed without direct negotiation of any kind with J.

We are confident we can bring about a satisfactory conclusion to proceedings that will enable you to move on with your life.

April

You'd started opening my mail. Sometimes, you'd stolen it. I knew this because I'd ordered a set of bank statements to the flat – they wouldn't send them anywhere but my registered address – and they'd never arrived. I re-ordered them: nothing. And then I'd phoned the bank and begged and pleaded, and eventually someone kind had made a special dispensation to have them sent to Zed's house and – miraculously! – they'd arrived the next day. Then the car got towed from outside the house and when I phoned the car pound, incandescent with anger, they told me I'd been sent several letters informing me the tax needed renewing. You'd taken them, too. And you must also have taken the car insurance renewal which I subsequently didn't pay, which meant that I drove around illegally for weeks, unwittingly, until I called up to add Zed to the policy and was told I no longer had one.

You were brazen enough to leave the less interesting bits of my post lying where you'd read them, envelopes torn, no effort to cover your tracks.

All of these things helped me come to dislike you more, little by little, day by day, week by week. It was a comforting, leaden sensation, a black place inside my chest that sometimes expanded, sometimes contracted, but never left me. I marvelled at it, this transference of feeling from light to dark. At times, I quite enjoyed its presence. It was different from the rage and panic and the distress: it was a quiet shift into seeing you for who you are, and what you have done. It was much, much easier.

And so when I heard the heavy envelope drop on the doormat that morning, I raced downstairs to see what had arrived. I noted your name on the envelope. I saw your lawyer's postmark on the back. And I ripped it open and devoured the contents inside, not caring even for a second that what I was doing was wrong. Hell, it was illegal. I'd made the point to your lawyers myself in several emails I'd written asking that you Stop Fucking Stealing My Mail. But this was better than all the things of mine you'd intercepted just to fuck me around a bit. This was the insider track on your war-room plotting. The whole transcript, no less. It gave me a kick that you'd gone to such trouble to plot against me, only to be so fucking stupid as to have the evidence hand-delivered to the house on a day you wouldn't be there. I almost felt bad for you.

Almost.

So now I knew your gameplay. It didn't make much difference, knowing the steps you'd planned. Erica Jong had already talked me through them, and reassured me that they weren't as terrifying as they sounded. But I was glad to have the heads-up on the derisory offer that would also be delivered through the door later that same day. Apportioning me less than a quarter of the value of the house in full and final settlement. I assumed your strategy was to price me out of London altogether so you could continue to peddle your twisted version of events without the inconvenience of me in the picture, however peripherally. Maybe you pictured me in a bedsit in Morecambe, slowly decaying like the town around me, bamboozled by your brilliant strategising.

I was no longer driven by that desperation to speak to you, to have my say, to talk you round. I saw, finally, the futility of that hope that you would relent. I saw myself as you saw me: a person you would never want to meet. A person you wouldn't be able to look in the eye. A person that had found you out, at last.

The thought of being in a courtroom with you hung over me now, making me tense, skittish. I was useless at work, and a dullard at play, going over and over the likely chain of events with friends on nights out meant to distract me from you. They were sympathetic enough, but I could tell they just wanted it over with. For my sake, and for their own. They'd had to listen to this shit for a long time now.

When I'd emptied the flat of my belongings, I'd been scrupulously fair about dividing what we shared, only breaking my own rule when I came to pack up the books.

Apart from that other, notable exception.

I didn't know what to do about that leaf I'd taken out of your dining table. It was a theft which was mitigated by my temporary insanity at the time – thinking you'd drop the ice-queen act and speak to me, in exchange for a piece of high-quality oak? I must have been quite out of my mind.

But I worried about having it in my possession. It sat gathering dust in my storage unit, that room of doom: a reminder of how much I had lost myself. I recalled the madder elements of my bad behaviour over Christmas and New Year. In giving in to my anger at you, I had lost my sense of morality, my sense of shame. I had been a monster. Not in the way you ever described but in ways I now felt mortified to recall. I remembered moving your things around, breaking them, hiding them. A truly pathetic attempt to insert myself into your consciousness, however negatively the impact would be felt. I realised that raging sense of injustice had burned out. The fire you'd lit in me by your refusal to talk had finally extinguished. I no longer cared to hear your thoughts, or tell you mine. I knew, now, that it no longer mattered. Neither of us made any sense to the other any more. It was a loss I had learned to live with.

*

And so the spring progressed as this dysfunctional year juddered forward. I could feel myself coming back together, using the space afforded by my stay at Zed's flat to process, to grieve, to reassess my life and rebuild it around the hole our marriage had left behind. I was the replicant in *Terminator 2*, slowly recongealing, standing my full height, becoming complete. Weird, I admit. But the image worked, somehow, when I called it to mind. I needed to imagine myself as surviving. I'd spent a long time feeling that I was fading away.

I started to hang out with friends again. Most of them. Some I knew were still in contact with you, and I felt this as a bitter betrayal. I knew how those nights out with them would play out. You would make yourself small, even smaller than you were, and look sad and hurt. You would brush over the gaps in your story to leave just a suggestion of wrongdoing, a whisper of violence. Filling in the details would have been too much: they would have baulked at that unreality. I confronted one or two of them, sending emails that spelled out what you'd said, what had been done. But they protested that they weren't taking sides, they were just making sure we were both OK.

It wasn't good enough. I cut them out.

I attempted a Tinder date, but knew at its end that I wasn't quite ready to 'move on' when I'd gone to shake the hand of the fresh-faced, pretty young thing who'd moved to kiss me, face expectantly upturned. I was more embarrassed than she was by my awkward departure, feeling at once both terribly old and highly amused by my own incompetence. I decided to give women a miss from then on, realising for the first time in my life that I wasn't actually interested in sex – or rather, the pursuit of it. You had killed the romance in me.

I felt the loss of this, but also the relief of not caring. I was very happy in my own company. The loss was greater for my friends, who were sorry I would not be adding to the rich seam of comedy my brief stint in the dating game had offered them. They pleaded with me to try again, hoping for more humiliations.

Every misadventure is a golden anecdote, just as soon as you're ready to tell it.

The appointment for our court date came through, and I was un-surprised to see it fall the day before our wedding anniversary. Of course. The universe itself wanted to emphasise the pathos of this whole shoddy affair. I had to spend hours typing up the paperwork that was required of me: a brief to my barrister, setting out what had been offered, what had been argued. A chronology of our lives together that countered your cruel and dishonest retellings. I was exhausted by it all. And I knew that, come what may, I'd be in the same room as you in just a few days' time and I could not reconcile the feelings that provoked in me. Anger and terror and excitement and, stupidly, hope. But mainly sadness, knowing that such hope was futile.

My sister phoned me to insist she would come with me on the day of the hearing. I pretended to resist, but was so grateful to have her support. We met at a Caffè Nero on High Holborn on the allotted day, both a little white in the face: me with anxiety, her because of the early start. Like me, she found what we were about to go through completely surreal. We laughed, just a tiny bit, about whether you'd turn up with a fake black eye. But mainly we were tense, watchful and intimidated. It was a relief when Erica Jong turned up and took over the role of my protector.

In the end, it took less than half a day to bring our entanglement to an end.

Erica arrived carrying a huge bundle of files, the fruits of my la-bour over the past few weeks, and greeted my sister and then me in the side room we'd taken occupation of when we'd arrived at court. It was a weird system: arriving first, we bagsied the best room, and I took a tiny crumb of satisfaction from our having got there ahead of you, knowing the room you were left with had just one tiny win-dow – ours had four! An early win.

We had some time before our court session. Was it as nerve-wracking for you as it was for me? Perhaps more? After all, you had a clear idea of what you wanted to get out of the day: as much as you possibly could. I was just there to stand up for myself against that. I hadn't actually considered what I was asking for.

It was a good job, then, that Erica was there. And my sister. She saw you, didn't she, when she went to the loo early on in the day? She didn't know how to react. Apparently you'd looked at her with your sad, hurt face, already arranged for the role of 'victim'. She came back to the room a bit shaken, castigating herself for giving you the cold shoulder – it wasn't like her to be rude, or offish. I stared at her as she worried about it, wondering why she hadn't tried to land one on you. 'I'm glad you didn't smile at her,' was the most measured I could be. 'It would have undermined me, and vindicated her.'

Shortly after, we were called in before the judge. Absurdly, it hadn't occurred to me that the action would take place in a court-room. It looked like a film set: there was the judge's bench, witness box and another long bench, behind which you sat with your team on the left, and me with Erica on the right. It was the first time I'd seen you in months. You, your solicitor and your barrister filed in just ahead of us, taking your seats without casting a single glance in our direction. The judge's bench was straight ahead. I looked over at you but you stayed stock-still, staring ahead. You were carrying the bag I'd bought you for your birthday last year. It made me angry: I didn't want you to have anything of mine, even something I'd gifted. Why the fuck would you have it still, if I was such a monster? It was OK to keep the material reminders, if you liked them enough – just erase every other thing and move on, right?

My heart was racing. I couldn't stop looking across at you. Erica nudged my elbow, motioning to me to look ahead just as the judge entered the room. It was all so utterly bizarre. A courtroom drama that I was actually in. None of it seemed in any way real.

The judge opened proceedings, and invited your barrister to put forward their opening argument. And then it began: another breathtaking betrayal. That I was on benefits when we'd met, that I'd hurried you into buying a flat so I could stop paying for a rental, that you'd shouldered the burden of all our finances while we were to-gether, and that now it was time you got your fair share. I couldn't believe it. I hadn't expected that your narrative would sink even lower.

Erica half turned to me, one eyebrow raised. I whispered furious-ly in her ear: I earned tax credits, it's hardly the same as being on the fucking dole. I put her up in my flat for months without asking for a penny, and then we both chose to make the next step into buying to-gether. I BUILT THE FUCKING FLAT. That was my contribution.

Erica put her hand on my knee, nodding. She wasn't fazed in the slightest. I guess she'd seen worse. She scribbled a few notes down and continued to listen intently. Then it was her turn to stand and address the judge. She calmly and quietly recited the facts of our marriage: your leaving, what the flat had been worth at purchase, what it was worth now. Our agreement that I would put a hold on my career in order to create a home for us, and that in spite of earn-ing less, I contributed equally to our finances. That your career had progressed as a result of my commitment to taking care of all do-mestic matters. That you could earn even more, since you were cur-rently only working part time.

And there, at last: she had provoked a response. I saw you quietly snort and roll your eyes. You couldn't help it. How dare she chal-lenge the saintly version of you, capable of keeping only the hours that you did – and no more – because your commitment within that time was so total, your devotion so unflinching? I smiled to myself. I couldn't help it. What cognitive dissonance must ring around your head, so great is the disparity between your view of yourself and what is actually real?

I looked down quickly, avoiding the judge's quizzical look. Short-ly after, she dismissed us all, with the instruction that hammering out an agreement now would be in all parties' best interests. There was a hint of contempt in her voice. She must have seen hundreds of cases like ours, desperate embittered people squabbling over a few thousand pounds. She said she was clear the case wasn't 50/50, which sent a shudder through me: but she also indicated that it could, at trial, be settled at something nearer to parity than the 75/25 I'd been offered. I looked up at her, and thought I saw her soften, just a little. Perhaps she understood what had just taken place. Perhaps she could see, too, that you weren't who you said you were.

Erica and I returned to our side room, where I told my sister what had happened as best I could. I was incoherent. Erica looked surprised. It was hard to explain how devastating it was to see your wife simply ignore your existence, before setting her team upon you to rip you limb from limb. If I was being dramatic, I didn't care. I hadn't prepared myself for the possibility you'd tell more lies. The gloves were off, and I hadn't yet landed a single punch.

She's an absolute shocker, said my sister, putting her arm around my shoulder and pulling me close. Don't take any notice. Stay calm. Look at what's really happening: she's had to pay those lawyers thousands of pounds to be here defending her. You're here on the cheap, because you're in the right. And when we leave, we'll go together and we'll have a drink and we'll be OK. And she'll be alone. How sad is that? She'll just leave, on her own, and stay that way. Probably forever.

That made me stop still. She was absolutely right. I hadn't asked for any of this, but I'd been sucked into it nonetheless. And it was mad. I was in court for the second time in a year – I'd never been to court in my life before. I had a barrister for fuck's sake. And I spent every waking minute calculating and recalculating how this would all play out, sending myself mad over percentages and projections.

It was a chaos all of your making – so typically you. Creating havoc all around while you sat, impregnable, in the centre. But I didn't have to sit with you any more. I didn't have to engage. I could let Erica negotiate and then I could leave, and that would be it. I knew that a tiny part of me had been holding onto this battle as a way of holding onto us. While it remained, I still had something of you, however grotesque. I didn't want there to be nothing at all.

But I also knew that staying in this was no longer an option. I had to end it today, no matter what would transpire in the course of these negotiations. Going to trial would most likely kill me.

Erica gave me a reassuring wink, which I saw my sister intercept with a grin, and left the room to meet with your barrister. Their discussions to bring our life together to an end would take place in the corridor outside. It seemed appropriately shabby.

You'd got all your figures wrong, of course. Erica came back in to check them with me, rolling her eyes as I rewrote the numbers against what the house would sell for, what we owed on the mortgage, what cut the estate agent would take. How on earth does she get by? she exclaimed.

She had me.

Well she doesn't any more. I'll be right back — these sums are great, thank you.

Minutes later, she returned. They're offering you a third, she'll take two-thirds. What do you think?

It was more than you'd ever put forward throughout this whole horrible ordeal. You must have been worried. I could feel the tide turning in my favour, and for a moment it made me greedy. Why settle for a third? I should go for half; it was more than I deserved after what you'd put me through. And it was only right: we'd been partners, we'd been married. We still were. An equal split was what I was owed.

My sister looked at me, sensing what I was thinking.

She paid the deposit, you remember. I know you did all the work, but this gives her back that money and you get a greater share of the profit you made on the flat, which was all your doing. It's fair, you know.

I knew. I did a quick calculation. It would give me enough for a decent place, maybe somewhere near Zed. It would be nice to make a move somewhere new. I knew I had to leave the neighbourhood. Running into you as I went about my daily routine would make my life unliveable.

Erica went back out of the room and I paced the floor, wondering what you were doing in your little cell across the corridor. Did you see, yet, that you'd imprisoned yourself along with me in this hellish place? Had you relented even a little, or were you feeling aggrieved as your team persuaded you to get out while the going was good?

The door opened again and Erica shot in, grinning. I pushed them to 65/35 – I felt you were owed a little something more for your trouble.

She was pleased with herself. It's not much, but I like to get a little extra so I cover my own fee.

I wanted to kiss her, but thought better of it, settling for a gormless smile and a thumbs up. Cool. Like the Fonz. We have to go back into the chamber now, and the judge will sign it off and then we're all done.

Just like that.

We waited for almost an hour before we were called back into the courtroom. And this time, there was a bottleneck outside the door as the occupants from the previous case were still leaving as we arrived. Suddenly, you appeared as well, and this time you couldn't avoid meeting my eye. At last, I had your attention. I knew this was my only chance to communicate directly, to show you what I was feeling. And so I kept your gaze, staring steadily into your eyes as I slowly, almost imperceptibly, shook my head from side to side. I saw you see me for the first time. And I saw you look away. You knew what you had done was shameful. But just like that, you put your mask back on and we filed into the room.

Within an hour I was sitting with my sister in a nearby bar, blinking at a cold glass of wine, feeling shell-shocked. We'd sent Erica off with a tight hug each, and profuse thanks. She was happy with her work, and we were absolutely delighted with her.

Time to start making plans, my sister said. She was right. It was a very weird adjustment. I wouldn't have to spend my time reacting to you any more. And I didn't just mean in relation to our divorce. I'd spent the past six years making plans based on what you wanted me to do. Now I was free. What on earth was I going to do?

You know it's our wedding anniversary tomorrow, I said.

My sister knew. She'd been avoiding mentioning it.

You've just got to forget you ever met her now. Put it all behind you. She's a mistake you made. Leave her in the past.

It was tough love. I probably needed to hear it. But beyond that, I was just too tired to take any more. So we drank, and we talked about other things, and we phoned my mum who'd been wracked with nerves just as we had been. She was relieved it was all over. She shared my sister's views of who and what you were.

We didn't stay out long. My sister had to travel north to slot back into her busy, fulfilling life. I had to carve out one of my own now, too. I headed back to Zed's and sat for a long time, with a drink, staring out of the window in the living room, across the Camden skyline to the Roundhouse in the distance. I was free. It was over, at last.

I woke up feeling the same heavy weight of dread that had greeted me every morning since you left. I got myself together and got to work, and was so busy all day I didn't think about what the date was. I left the office at nearly 7 p.m., and on my walk to the tube I considered that three years ago to the day, we had been married. The thought of this made me change direction, switching to the route that would pass by where you worked, knowing that your clinic was now just the other side of the Elephant. I told myself it was a test: now that it was all over, I should be strong enough to manage the prospect of running into you.

And I knew, deep down inside me, that I would.

I don't know what had given me such strong prescience that our paths would cross. Perhaps the drama – or the romance – of it being our anniversary. Perhaps I thought about it happening more days than I cared to admit, but it was only that day I'd been right.

I stopped absolutely still as I saw you coming out of the revolving doors. You didn't see me at first, so I moved towards you, smiling. A genuine smile, but it flummoxed you completely.

Get out of my way, I'm in a rush.

It's really nice to see you too! Hey, just wait a second. It's me, you remember? You know what today is?

You did, I could tell; it made you slow down, almost to a standstill. But not quite. I ploughed on.

How are you? Can we talk? It's all over now, and you always said you'd talk to me when it was over. Can we talk? Can we make a time?

I'm busy now, my mum's not well.

You clamped shut your mouth, not wanting to share even this much of yourself.

I've got to go.

I was concerned. I still had a soft spot for your mum, in spite of everything. I offered to do something, not really knowing what I meant. I didn't want you to have to deal with it by yourself. Standing in front of you in real life, for the first time in months, I assumed the role I'd always taken: I tried to help you. And then I said something totally unguarded, leaving you absolutely flummoxed.

'I just want to give you a hug.'

It was true. I hadn't realised it until I said it, but you looked so small and hassled and... angry. Like a stroppy child who can't stop their tantrum, even though she's only making herself unhappy.

Of course, you weren't up for it.

I changed tack, trying once again to set a date, a time when we might talk. I said that, if nothing else, shouldn't the coincidence of us seeing each other today, of all days, persuade you that there was something between us? Something to salvage?

But you'd already started walking. So I let you go and asked that you wish your mother well from me. Idiot. And then I said sorry. I said sorry for all the petty, shitty things I had done since you left. And before. I meant every word. But you didn't hear, I don't think. You were already turning the corner.

The sale of the house moved closer. I dreaded as well as longed for the day it would be completed, the keys handed back, the money in my account. What would I do with it? I had grown used to living in a state of suspended animation, moving neither forward nor back. Existing. Switching from friend's place to friend's place, my belongings safely stored in a warehouse down by the riverside. I had to start making concrete plans. I knew it would be good for me to look to the future. Investing in a new home, my own space, would be a very good start. Zed would be back before long so it was time I got my arse in gear.

You were all sorted, I knew that. I'd seen the estate agents' brochures left pointedly on the kitchen table. A final attempt to hurt me. You were way ahead of me, as usual; you'd been ready to move before I'd even fully realised you'd gone.

I started to look at some property details, and I made a decision to move away from our neighbourhood. It was partly out of necessity: the gentrification that had added so much value to our flat meant I was priced out anyway. Besides, I was really over the hipster invasion. The list of options in the endless number of cafés now sprawled across the area made me anxious.

I remembered New Year's Eve, and blinking back tears at our neighbour's party as a very drunk Irish woman extolled the virtues of living in Tottenham. I smiled at the memory. And then I got on a bus and had a look round the area, and before I knew it, I had a new plan.

It was hard, still, to let the flat go. On the day before the sale completed, I had to go back: I wanted to check there was nothing left of mine to take with me. Besides, your lawyer had inserted a clause into our settlement agreement that made me responsible for cleaning before the keys were handed over. I hadn't noticed at the time – I was a bit distracted during that awful morning in court – but it was classic you: literally getting someone else to do your dirty work.

I'd considered pushing back but knew you'd only leave the flat in a mess if I didn't do it, and I wanted its new occupants to see it at its best. I still felt a proud attachment to it: I wanted them to love it as much as I did.

Besides, you'd have no fucking clue where the cleaning stuff was.

So I headed over to say goodbye. I knew it would hurt. I had imagined us spending years together in that flat. Successions of birthdays and Christmases and parties and quiet nights in together. New jobs, new friends, new ideas. The arrival of children. The departure of parents. Facing it all here together, us two in our little sanctuary. It wasn't just a house I was saying goodbye to: it was a future that I was never going to have.

I put my key in the door and for a split second, I imagined I could hear your voice. I felt a rush of warmth as I allowed myself to believe you were inside, waiting for me. I climbed the stairs in a hurry, arriving in the kitchen in a fluster of noise and motion. An empty kitchen. An empty flat. I took one last look around, superimposing onto each room my memories of furniture now removed, fixtures taken down, photographs destroyed.

There was nothing left behind. You'd even emptied the loft of the few things I'd left behind in there. I dusted and hoovered and polished. I left everything looking as good as I could. I kept my side of the bargain.

Finally, I sat down and wrote one last letter. I wanted to leave you this memento in paper and ink. I was done with email, done with texting. You might take this and shred it, or burn it, or toss it into a bin. But you would have held it in your hand, and you would have felt the weight of me in its pages. And maybe, just maybe, you would keep it and remember me and, in time, remember what you did and what really transpired between us.

Maybe.

Hello.

It is now many months since you left me. Many months in which I have attempted to contact you, to speak with you, to understand what you want and how I can help you have it. I struggle every day to cope with the fact of you simply disappearing from my life. It doesn't fit with who I am.

But I don't want these feelings of pain, of despair, of anger. They are yours to hold, not mine.

After you left, I wanted us to be kind. I thought we could build a future that was separate, but happy. I said this over and over. In return you blocked contact by phone, ignored emails and refused meetings. You did this because you felt ashamed of the lies you'd told and the things you'd done. I understand that. It is not surprising.

It is your right to ignore me. To clinically excise me from your life as you have. I was hurt beyond words by your doing this. I remain devastated by the lack of care, the lack of respect this shows me.

I know this pattern of behaviour in you is one you have repeated many times. Perhaps you are not fully conscious of it. Perhaps you are, and it suits you to defend yourself in this way. But you didn't need to defend yourself from me. I had held you for many years. I hoped you would see I could have continued to do this, even as your friend. I hoped you'd see it before you trashed everything beyond all repair.

I am not abusive and controlling. No one is convinced by this narrative (with the sorry exception of your sister).

I loved you. And love is never controlling. It is never conditional. It is always honest. It doesn't bargain. I don't think you can love like this. You have never seen love like this. I tried so hard to love you like this, and to fulfil those unmet needs that you carry deep down inside you.

I don't understand where you buried the feelings that we shared for each other, but I accept that I cannot make you process any of this. I have had to do this for and by myself.

At times, I have tried to forget you, simply so I could get through the day. It was exhausting. The effort nearly killed me. But my memories of our happy times together have held, and for this reason it hurts me to think of you feeling sad or alone. I understand you. I know you will be hurting. This brings me no pleasure.

You can – you should, you must – do better than this.

Please meet me halfway, and let's build that friendship. It's up to you now: there is a future for us to share, you only have to reach out towards me. But you should know that it is no longer my loss if you do not.

I bear you no grudge. I hope that in time you will be happy, as I now am. I hope you will see clearly what we were, as I now can.

I will always remember you. I know you will always remember me...

With love.

J

PS. I have a leaf of your table. I'd like to give it back.

An empty house is a soulless, desolate place. I left it behind, carrying the letter for you in my hand. I would drop it to your lawyer in the morning.

What a terrible ending to a marriage.

Epilogue

It took me many months to give up on you. To lose all hope of you relenting. To finally realise that you hadn't acted out of character during our divorce: you'd acted out of character when we'd come together.

The real you had been there all along, I just hadn't seen her.

It was like recovering from an illness: the symptoms gradually disappear but the rebuilding of strength, the regaining of muscle mass and resilience and immunity... that takes much longer.

Zed came back from overseas, and helped me scope out a new place to live. It made me laugh that, six months on from that New Year's Eve when I'd been reduced to tears by the suggestion of moving to Tottenham, I found myself pounding the streets of N15. It was strange that, although I was buying on my own this time, the process felt the same as when we'd bought our place. In fact, I felt more supported: Zed was engaged and involved and enthusiastic. I didn't feel on my own any more. It shocked me to realise how long I had felt alone, when I was with you.

I found a house on a terraced street that I could just about afford if I borrowed as much as the bank would allow. It was a shithole, of course, but I knew I could fix it up. In spite of what you'd said in court, I was a seasoned renovator now, and I was ready to get cracking on another build.

Slowly, little by little, the ties that bound me to my life with you were loosened, and then undone. I got to know a new neighbourhood, and felt glad rather than sorry that I had made the move out of ours. I would revisit from time to time to see friends and noticed that I no longer felt a pang of loss.

Once, walking down the high street, I saw two men that I recognised but could not place. They were sitting outside the cinema, drinking cider on the pavement. I stared at them from across the street for a long time before it clicked: they were the homeless men that had helped our useless wedding driver get the bus out onto the road from in front of the town hall. The two that had featured in our wedding album, that we'd laughed about together. In another time, another place. I smiled, and crossed the street to give them some money.

It didn't hurt me. Not any more.

All my belongings remained in storage. I lived in my new house among the rubble and the chaos, spending long evenings stripping floors, putting up partition walls, pulling down Artex ceilings. It was exhausting, but it was progress.

There were few connections left between us, but one mutual friend told me gently that they'd been to see you, spending the evening in your new home. She showed me a photo of your living room, filled with the pictures and furniture and knick-knacks that I'd once come home to. And a new dining table.

I wobbled. It was distressing to see your life continuing without me in it. And it made me sadder than I could say that you'd bought a new table.

I couldn't explain why.

There weren't many moments like this. The mutual friends we had would, over time, separate into my camp or yours. You retained one or two of the group who'd known you a lot longer than me, and who I wouldn't miss. And anyway, I wanted you to have friends. I was glad that a couple of people stuck around for you. At first I felt it as a condemnation: that they must have heard all you'd said about me and concluded it was true. But I think now that you just didn't tell them what you were up to. Secrecy and lies underpinned our relationship. Why wouldn't they underpin these others of yours, too?

I saw how it would go, your telling of our story. A selective recap of my worst bits embellished with some of the highlights of your abuse narrative – but not too much. You wouldn't overgild the lily, and risk being questioned too deeply about what had transpired. You'd hint darkly at things, you'd become tearful, you'd demur. I could see it play out very clearly in my mind's eye. And so I didn't mind, in the end, that a couple of people seemed to take your side. I thought them deceived, just as I had been. More fool them.

I spent a testing evening with a friend who told me they couldn't take sides over what had transpired between us because they had been raised by divorced parents. I held my tongue, and smiled inwardly at the wasted investment they'd made in decades of analyses and talking treatments. So much for therapy.

But mainly I learned to navigate these less intimate friendships with a light touch, rising above the stabs of indignation that you weren't being held to task for what you had done to me.

You can't rely on other people to feel your outrage. To be invested in your distress. Other people's break-ups are hard to take.

My closer friends had to reconsider who you were, and what they had meant to you. You disappeared from their lives as you had mine. It was strange and sad for them, as well.

Little by little, I came down off the drug of you. I started to recognise the times and the ways that you'd tricked me, like a junkie getting clean, the clear-headedness of sobriety. During the past year I had crashed down, hard, from the high I'd created by idolising you for so long. I now had to find ways to feel happy without having my fix. I had to detoxify myself of you completely.

I started to regain my self-confidence. You had made me distrust my own instincts, my sense of who I was. I'd believed your version of me, for a while, but now I was getting myself back.

It was such a relief.

I came out of hiding. I started to have fun again. And then something happened, that I hadn't expected in a million years. I almost didn't let it.

There had been someone else, before you. Someone I'd fallen for, many years ago now, but nothing had ever come of it. I'd spent a long year trying to persuade her that we would be good together, that she should take a chance on us. But it had frightened her off. She wasn't like you. She didn't enjoy the arrogant, confident me that pinned you up against a wall and kissed you on our first night out together. I'd tried that move, and it had scared the life out of her.

Before you and I had got together, she had called an end to our protracted, painful non-courtship. I think it was my determination to get over her that had made me throw myself so totally into you. I told myself at the time that my absorption in us was because you were The One. I now think it's because you were The Rebound.

That sounds awful.

It's only partly true. I was still pining for her when we met, but I did fall for you. I'm not going to rewrite that history, to follow your lead in erasing all traces of what we were.

You were never comfortable when she was around. I didn't tell you the full story of me and her, but you were smart enough to know that there was unfinished business. You were frosty with her on those few occasions we'd met, at parties or, once, at a festival. But you dismissed your behaviour, acting like you'd done nothing different. You pretended you hadn't noticed her. You did an amazing job of showing me you cared about it while acting like you didn't care at all.

There had been one night, about a year after we met, that I'd been out on my own and run into her at a friend's place. She knew about me and you. She – finally! – realised that what we had had, however fledgling and unready, was something important. Something special.

And so she'd tried to kiss me, in the corridor outside the bathroom in our friend's house. I'd been so angry with her then. I'd waited so long for this show of passion, and she'd offered it only when it was too late.

I was surprised not to feel more thrown by it. But by then, you and I were solid; we'd made a commitment to each other and I was set on our path. I felt safe. I thought I knew what lay ahead for me and I was glad of it.

How different things would have been if I'd paused in that moment. If I'd acted on that kiss, renewed that feeling that I'd shut down so abruptly in the moment of meeting you. Could I have done it? I don't think I could. I had set my heart on our love story, and I didn't want to stain the pages of it.

I didn't see her again for a long time after that.

And then, suddenly, she was there. She had heard about what had happened. She was worried about me. She knew things were bad, and wanted to reach out. She wondered if I needed support.

And I did. I was glad to reconnect. I knew I wouldn't have to defend myself with her. She was on my side already. She knew me.

We went to a Thai restaurant and failed to eat as I told her the story. She looked at me wide-eyed as I went through your leaving, the cache of documents I'd found, the abuse narrative, the non-molestation order. The whole sordid tale.

I told myself that nothing could happen with her. I wasn't ready. She'd flaked out on me in the past, and I wasn't strong enough to let her do that to me again.

I repeated this mantra.

I tried to remain aloof.

I wasn't ready to trust someone.

I wasn't mended.

I wasn't sure.

I wasn't me.

And then one day, things changed.

Is this love?

Acknowledgements

I wrote this book for me. It didn't occur to me, for some time, that anyone else would read it. I'd like to thank the following people who did, and in doing so made it much, much better.

To my Primadonna sisters: I would not have had the audacity to write a novel without having first known and worked with you. Thanks to you all but in particular to Catherine Mayer for co-creating the world's best festival and for being the first reader of this book. Your gentle advice improved my story. Your friendship and support (and mad ideas that put me to work) improve my life. Also to Sabeena Akhtar and Amie Corry for reading early drafts, and for keeping me level-headed via WhatsApp. Thanks to Kit de Waal, to whom I first spoke out loud about the idea for this book, and who won't know that our conversation shaped its ending. And to Shona Abhyankar for your aggressive support, constant provocations and for introducing me to my wonderful agent. I owe you, big time.

To Sophie Lambert, my wonderful agent. Thank you for taking me on, and in so doing giving me one of the purest adrenalin rushes of my life. You are exactly how I imagined an agent would be – and how all agents should be.

Thank you to Hannah Westland for publishing this book – for being moved by it – and for your thoughtful feedback and careful editing. Thank you to everyone at Serpent's Tail who has helped in the process of getting it into print.

To my friends, who are also my family: Nic Godwin, I'm sorry you found the book upsetting, but I'm not sorry I asked you to read it. Caroline Clarke and Lady Vic: you helped shape it too, and for that as well as many drinks, I owe you. And to two wonderful best women, Nikki Stopford and Deb Googe: I hope I did you justice. I suspect you won't think I did.

To my family, who are also my home: thanks to my parents, my godmother and in particular my little sister Clare for getting me through this story.

Finally, and most of all, thank you to Natalie Koffman, who is love.

6|93

This book is to be returned on or before the date above.
It may be borrowed for a further period if not in demand.

COLCHESTER
LIBRARIES